Charlotte's Strip

Step-by-Step How-To's on Sewing for Dolls

Charlotte Semple

Copyright © 2024 by Charlotte Kantz-Semple

All rights reserved. No part of this publication may be reproduced, distributed, or transmitted in any form or by any means, including photocopying, recording, or other electronic or mechanical methods, without the prior written permission of the publisher, except in the case of brief quotations embodied in critical reviews.

ISBN 978-1-916606-47-0 (Paperback)

Illustrations by Charlotte Kantz-Semple

Book and Cover Design by PaperTrue Ltd.

Editing by PaperTrue Ltd.

Published in United States of America, 2024

Published by PaperTrue Ltd.
Market Street, Suite 1300, San Francisco, CA 94111

DEDICATION

For Audie, my grandmother, who taught me how to make my first stitch at age six. For my mum, who happily encouraged my sewing efforts and taught me how to use a sewing machine. For Fred, who dared me to strive beyond Loving Hands at Home. For Elsie, who impressed upon me that finishing reveals true couture. For Liz, who introduced me to the world of dolls. And for Margaret, my dearest friend, who encouraged me to "go for it!"

Acknowledgements

Creating a "how-to" book like this requires years of education, research, creativity, and teaching ability. My desire to share the knowledge and experience I have gained throughout the last 42 years of dollmaking is the catalyst behind this book.

A web of interconnectedness was essential to its completion. The enthusiastic support of the Doll Artisan Guild, my teachers, local doll clubs, my three children, the magazines that published my work, and my loyal clients guided me in this direction. Without them, I could not have completed this book, and I heartily thank them for their encouragement.

Introduction

The frustration of adapting generic patterns is outdated and unnecessary. The heart of this teaching manual is what I call Charlotte's Strip. It is an organizational tool, individualized for any doll, enabling users to create precise patterns.

Clearly written, step-by-step instructions guide readers as they work on developing patterns following the development of a Charlotte's Strip. Accurate and detailed drawings provide a visual understanding of the written instructions.

The book contains two parts. Part one is devoted to the development of the Charlotte's Strip and its use in creating well-fitting patterns. In part two, I answer some of the many questions I received about sewing for dolls. Over the years, these questions have varied widely: how to adapt a drawers pattern for bloomers, how to sew a seam in a fur coat, what sewing techniques are best for lightweight fabric, and many more.

Some of the instructions and answers are lengthy but thorough. Bear with me. I guarantee you will be satisfied with the garments you produce. You might wonder about some of the measurements I ask you to make while developing your Charlotte's Strip and basic patterns. Don't worry—throughout my many years of sewing for dolls, the measurements I chose for pattern development have worked not only for my own dolls' apparel but also for those of many other dollmakers.

I hope you find this book instructive and interesting.

Contents

Charlotte's Strip	1
Step-by-Step How-To's on Sewing for Dolls	1
Dedication	3
Acknowledgements	4
Introduction	5
Contents	7
Charlotte's Strip	13
A DOLL'S CHARLOTTE'S STRIP	14
BODY MEASUREMENTS (ANY DOLL, ANY BODY)	14
Drafting a Pattern	21
BASIC SHAPES	21
FRONT BODICE BASIC SHAPE	22
BACK BODICE BASIC SHAPE	28
FRONT BODICE BASIC SHAPE WITH DART	34
BACK BODICE BASIC SHAPE WITH DART	35
SLEEVE BASIC SHAPE	38
DRAWERS BASIC SHAPE	41
Basic Patterns	45
DRAWERS	45
DRAWERS BASIC PATTERN	45
DRAWSTRING WAIST CASING	48
WAISTBAND-WAIST	50
HEM	52

SLIP	53
DROP-WAIST BODICE BASIC PATTERN	53
SLIP DROP-WAIST BODICE WITH DART BASIC PATTERN	58
DRESS	64
DROP-WAIST BODICE BASIC PATTERN	64
DROP-WAIST BODICE WITH DART BASIC PATTERN	69
SLEEVE BASIC PATTERN	75

Semple Answers to Questions on Sewing for Dolls — 79

A FEW NOTES:	79
SEWING CENTER SUPPLIES	80

On Patterns — 83

DRAWERS	83
KNEE DRAWSTRING	83
KNEE CUFF	85
UNDERWEAR TERMS	87
BREECHES	87
BRIEFS	87
DRAWERS	87
KNICKERBOCKERS	88
KNICKERS	88
PANTALOONS	88
BLOOMERS	88
PANTALETTES	89
SLEEVES	89
DRAWSTRING AT WRIST	89
CUFF AT WRIST	91
LACE TO WRIST	92
FULL CAP	93
ABOUT SLEEVE PATTERNS	95
NECKLINES	95
TOO TIGHT	95
TOO LARGE	97
COTTON-KNIT SOCKS	97
"A" DESIGN SLIP	99

On General Sewing — 103

SEWING DEFINITIONS	103
CUTTING LINE	103
SEAMLINE	103
SEAM ALLOWANCE	103

Underarm Seam	104
Running Stitch	104
Blanket Stitch	104
Buttonhole Stitch	104
Slipstitch	105
Back Stitch	106
Armscye	106
Mark Cut-on-Fold Lines Red	106
Basting	106
Sewing Machine Needles	107
Type	107
Snagging	107
Seams	108
Raw Edges	108
French	108
Backstitching	109
Hems	109
Treatment	109
Rolled	110
Threads	111
Gathering	111
Machine vs. Hand-Sewing	112
Tails and Tension	112
Pulling Threads	113
Hand-Sewing Length	114
Variety of Threads	114
Mercerized Cotton	114
Extra Strong Button and Carpet	114
Mercerized Cotton-Covered Polyester	114
Transparent Nylon	115
Rayon	115
Silver and Gold Metallic	115
Silk	115
Plackets	115
Ordinary	115
Simple	116
Really Lazy	117
Pressing	117
Pressing Cloth	117
Finger Pressing	118
Pleats	118
Knife Pleats	118

Box Pleats	119
Stacked Pleats	119
Rolled Pleats	120
Cartridge Pleats	120
Bumroll	121
Farthingale?	121
Tuck 'N Press Pleater	122
Pin-Tucks	122

On Fabrics — 124
Velveteen	124
Tulle	124
Brushed Felt	125
Fraying Velvet Edges	126
Seam Sticks	127

On Finishing — 128
Bias Piping	128
Trim	128
Lined	130
Unlined	130
Trimming Edges	134
Lace-Bound	134
Hand-Made Scallops	134
Machine-Sewn Scallops	135
Cut Scallops	135
Flat Lace Trim	136
Gathered Lace Trim	136
Finishing Terms	136
Lining	136
Interlining	136
Facing	136
Interfacing	137
Bias Binding	137

On Lace — 139
Lace Heading	139
Lace on Socks	140
Shaping Lace	140
On a Curve	140
Oval Panels	141
Shadow Panels	142

ENTREDEUX	143
WITH RUFFLE ATTACHED	143
ATTACHED TO AN EDGE	144

On Fasteners — 146

HISTORY	146
STRINGS AND RIBBONS	146
BUTTONS	146
HOOKS AND EYES	146
SNAP FASTENERS	147
SAFETY PINS	147
ZIPPERS	147
ELASTIC	147
LOOP BUTTONHOLES	147

On Leather And Fur — 150

SUEDE FABRIC	150
RABBIT PELT	151
FUR AS TRIM	152
PLUSH FABRIC SEAMS	153
LEATHER SHOES (FOR DOLLS)	154

Off The Cuff — 157

SEWING SILK	157
CUT-ON-FOLD	157
USING SPRAY-STARCH	157
USE THAT THIMBLE	157
HYDROGEN PEROXIDE	157
PATTERN NOTCHES	157
PIN AND BASTE	157
FAVORITE MUSIC	158
CHANGING NEEDLES	158
PINKING SHEARS FOR SOLES	158
IRONING BOARD PROTECTION	158
THREAD LENGTH	158
HIDING PIN HEADS	158
DOLLHOUSE DOLL SEWING	158
THIRD HAND	158
MAGNIFYING GLASS	159
NO RUST HERE	159
WASHING HANDS	159
TERRY CLOTH FOR LACE	159

SERGER TRIMS	159
YOUR BIG TOE	159
BIAS FABRIC SASHES	159
ALTERNATING HOOKS AND EYES	159
WRAPPING SPRAY-STARCHED PIECES	159
FULL NEEDLES AT THE READY	159
DON'T LIKE MAKING KNOTS?	160
LESS LACE IS BETTER	160
RIBBON CURLS	160
NAKED DOLLS IN STANDS	160
GLUING LAMBSKIN WIGS	160
VINEGAR SETS DYES	160
SEWING SCISSORS VS. PAPER SCISSORS	160
SEWING NEEDLES FOR LEATHER	160
CLEANING FEED DOGS	160
NO PRESSING LACE	161
EMERY BOARD REVISITED	161
KEEPING PINS CLEAN	161
SEWING PINS VS. CRAFT PINS	161
THIN SILK PINS ARE THE BEST	161
LEATHER FINGER GUARD	161
SPRAY-STARCH FABRIC FIRST	161
FRAY CHECK FOR HAND-MADE BUTTONHOLES	161
FABRIC GLUE IS GREAT!	161
DAMP PINS DON'T WORK	162
LONG 3-INCH PEARL HEAD PINS	162
SMALL STRING FOR DOLL PIPING	162
FRAY CHECK SOOTHES FRUSTRATIONS	162
PIPING FOR FINISHING	162
OUTER GARMENTS OVER UNDERGARMENTS	162
NO WRING, NO WRINKLE	162
DYEING FEATHERS	162
SMALL BRUSH FOR MACHINE EMBROIDERING	162
RULERS MAKE EVEN BIAS	162
DOLL-SIZED BUTTONS	162

Charlotte's Strip

When I first started sewing for dolls, I realized I needed something to help me keep track of each doll's various measurements. It was a chore to remeasure a doll's body, or that of a similar doll, every time I sewed for my own dolls or those of my clients. I started to make an organized strip for each doll, naming it Charlotte's Strip. This strip is a tool from which even a novice dollmaker can gather enough information to construct a complete outfit for a doll, confident that it will fit perfectly.

One question you might ask while making a Charlotte's Strip is, "Why did I choose **C** as the symbol for a doll's waistline?" I studied the piano from childhood well into my college years. Middle C is the center of the piano keyboard. Right? What does one think of as the center location of a doll's torso? The waist. So, for me, **C** represents a doll's torso waistline. Thus, it follows that I would use **E** for chest (empire), **H** for hips (naturally), **T** for thighs, **K** for knees, **N** for neck, **S** for shoulder, **U** for upper arm, **L** for elbow (I already used E, so why not L—sound it out, saying "eLbow"—hmm?), **W** for wrist, and so on. Then there are the questions about **A** and the two **B**s.

To develop the basic shapes from which the fundamental patterns were created, I needed a reference point along the center front line of the doll's torso. I chose the small "v" at the front center of a person's collarbone. Although a doll doesn't have a collarbone, I could create a reference point on the torso. Since **A** is the first letter of the alphabet, I decided to use it as the starting point for my measurements. Why use **B** for the finished hemline of both the under and outer garments? **B** follows **A**. Measuring from **A** to **B** for the length of a doll's finished hemlines made sense.

Why the two different **B**s? Let me explain. If a doll's dress and slip skirt are the same length, the dress skirt will appear slightly shorter than the slip skirt when on the doll. This happens because the dress skirt tends to press the slip skirt against the doll's legs, making the slip skirt appear longer. Oh, horrors! No doll wants her "secret" to show.

After experimenting with various dress and slip skirt lengths, I discovered that if a dress skirt is at least 1/4 inch (6mm) longer than the slip skirt, both skirts will appear even, keeping a doll's "secret" a secret. Therefore, **B1** represents the hem length of the finished outer garment, and **B2** represents the hem length of the finished undergarment.

A doll's secret? Of course. Even we humans don't want our undergarments to show, so why would a doll? The sewing label I attach to any doll's undergarments I make has "A Bébé's Secret" printed on it.

Follow me here and learn how to make a Charlotte's Strip for each of your dolls. Be sure to have at least one doll "in nature" nearby. You'll need some clean paper, a clear plastic ruler, a sharp pencil, a black pen *(not a permanent marker)*, a small pair of scissors, tape, a few thin straight pins, and a measuring tape.

Let's get started.

A Doll's Charlotte's Strip

Body Measurements (Any Doll, Any Body)
Refer to *Fig.1-1* and *Fig.1-2 as* examples while developing a your doll's Charlotte's Strip.

Fig.1-1 is an example of a Charlotte's Strip.

Fig.1-2 shows where to take the measurements on a doll's body for including in its Charlotte's Strip.

Note: The following instructions are primarily for a composition or bisque doll body. Additional instructions for cloth or leather body will be in *italics*.

For your reference, **red** ink represents pencil lines/marks in the Line Drawings (Fig.).

A black pen (no pencil) is used to make all marks, lines, measurements, and remarks on your strip.

Have some fun with this.

1. Cut a piece of clean paper 4 inches (10cm) wider and 1 inch (3cm) longer than your doll's body. If you have a large doll, you might need to tape two or more paper strips together to achieve the required length.

   Why the 4-inch width? Simply because I store my dolls' strips and patterns in #10 envelopes—which are 4.124 inches wide—and thought you might do the same.

2. Place the strip on a flat surface with the long edges facing left and right. Draw a vertical line 1/2 inch (1cm) from the left edge down the length of the paper, starting 2 inches (5cm) from the top. This is the beginning of your doll's Charlotte's Strip.

3. Measure your doll's body from its center back neck socket edge to where the heels touch a flat surface. This is the body's length, which will help you determine the length of your doll's

Charlotte's Strip. Indicate the doll's length at the top of the strip, along with the dollmaker (e.g., Bru, Steiner, Kestner, etc.) and the type of doll body (e.g., French, German, Modern, composition, bisque, leather, cloth). *(Fig.1-1)*

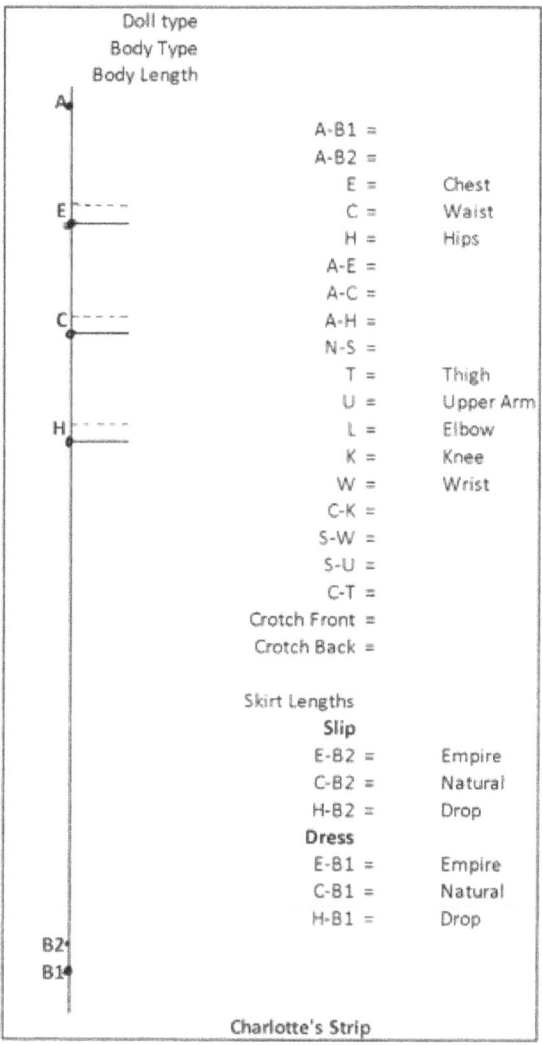

Fig.1-1

4. On the strip, make a large dot at the top of the line (in the left 1/2-inch margin). Label this dot as **A**. This represents the center front neck edge of your doll's torso, analogous to the little "v" in the center of your own collarbone. *(Fig.1-1)*

5. Make a pencil mark on your doll's torso at the center front neck socket edge. Consider this mark as **A**. *(Fig.1-2)*

For cloth-bodied dolls without a shoulder plate, use a fabric marker or a straight pin to mark where the center of the doll's collarbone might be.

For a cloth- or leather-bodied doll with a shoulder plate, use the pencil and your best imagination to mark where the center of the doll's collarbone might be.

Pencil marks on composition or bisque are easily washed away. Fabric marker marks on cloth or leather will eventually fade. I wouldn't use straight pins in leather bodies.

From here on, I will refer to your doll's Charlotte's Strip as "your doll's strip," rather than write out "your doll's Charlotte's Strip" every time I mention it. OK?

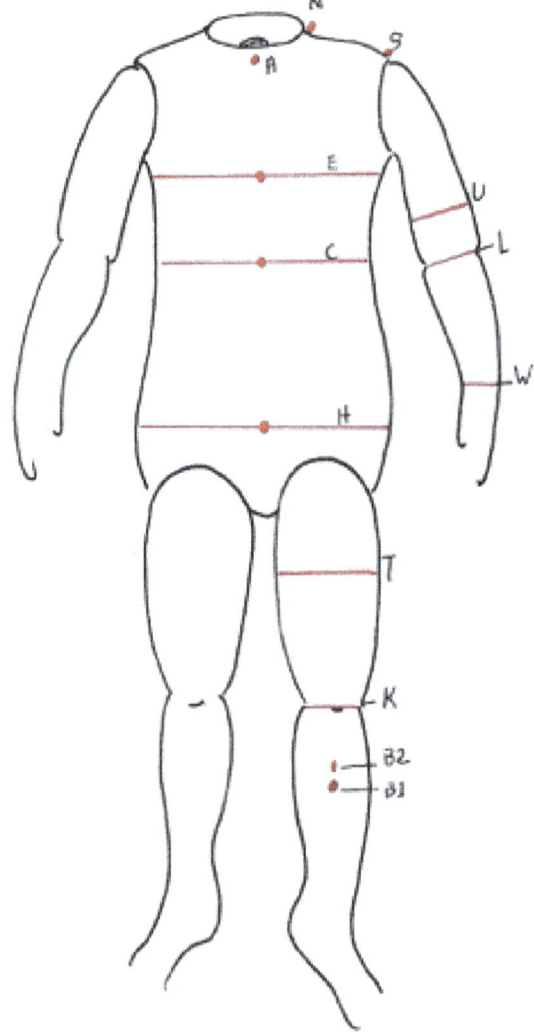

Fig.1-2

6. From this mark (**A**), measure where you want your doll's finished outer garment hem to fall. Make a light pencil mark on the doll's leg. Most Bébé dolls represent young girls and boys who would not wear long garments, so their finished garment hems would fall mid-shin level or slightly below the knee. *(Fig.1-2)*

Use either a fabric marker or a straight pin for a cloth-bodied doll. For a leather-bodied doll, use a fabric marker.

7. Transfer this measurement onto the vertical line on your doll's strip, making a large dot at the end of the measurement and labeling it as **B1**. *(Fig.1-1)*

8. Make a smaller dot on the line 1/4 inch (6mm) above **B1**. Label this smaller dot as **B2**. **B2** represents where your doll's finished undergarment hem will fall. Indicate these measurements on the right side of your doll's strip as **A-B1**=___ and **A-B2**=___. *(Fig.1-1)*

9. Cut a long narrow piece of paper about 1/8 inch (3mm) wide. Fit it snugly around the narrowest part of your doll's torso waist. Tape it in place where it overlaps. Draw a light pencil line around the waist where the bottom edge of the paper touches the torso. *(Fig.1-2)*

Mark a cloth body with either straight pins or a fabric marker. Mark a leather body with a fabric marker.

10. Carefully cut the paper away and measure it. This is the natural waist measurement of your doll's torso. Indicate this measurement on your doll's strip as **C**=___. *(Fig.1-1)*

11. Make a pencil dot at the center front of the waist pencil line **C** on your doll's torso. *(Fig.1-2)*

Mark a cloth body with either the fabric marker or a straight pin. Mark a leather body with the fabric marker.

12. Measure from the pencil dot at the center front neck edge (**A**) to the pencil dot at the center front waist (**C**) on your doll's torso. Transfer this measurement onto your doll's strip, starting from **A**. Make a large dot at the end of this measurement. Label this as **C**. Indicate this measurement on your doll's strip as **A-C**=___. *(Fig.1-1)*

13. Draw a 1/2-inch (1cm) solid line to the right of dot **C** on your doll's strip. Draw a 1/2-inch dotted line 1/4 inch above the solid line at dot **C**. *(Fig.1-1)*

14. Cut another narrow piece of paper to fit around your doll's torso and hips. Tape it in place where it overlaps. Draw a light pencil line around the hips where the bottom edge of the paper touches the torso. *(Fig.1-2)*

Mark a cloth body with either straight pins or the fabric marker. Mark a leather body with the fabric marker.

15. Carefully cut the paper away from the body and measure it. This is the natural hip, or drop, measurement (**H**) of your doll's torso. Indicate this measurement on your doll's strip as **H**=___. *(Fig.1-1)*

16. Make a pencil dot at the center front of the hip pencil line **H** on your doll's torso. *(Fig.1-2)*

    Mark a cloth body with either straight pins or the fabric marker. Mark a leather body with the fabric marker.

17. Measure from the pencil dot at the center front neck edge (**A**) to the pencil dot at the center front hip line (**H**) on your doll's torso. Transfer this measurement onto your doll's strip, starting from **A**. Make a large dot at the end of this measurement. Mark this dot as **H**. Indicate this measurement on the right side of your doll's strip as **A-H**=___. *(Fig.1-1)*

18. Draw a 1/2-inch solid line at dot **H** to the right of the line on your doll's strip. Draw a 1/2-inch dotted line 1/4 inch above the solid line at dot **H**. *(Fig.1-1)*

19. Cut another narrow piece of paper to fit around your doll's torso's chest at armpit level. Tape it in place where it overlaps. Draw a light pencil line around the chest where the bottom edge of the paper touches the torso. *(Fig.1-2)*

    Mark a cloth body with either straight pins or the fabric marker. Mark a leather body with the fabric marker.

20. Carefully cut the paper away from the body and measure it. This is the natural chest (**E**), or empire, measurement of your doll's torso. Indicate this measurement on your doll's strip as **E**=___. *(Fig.1-1)*

21. Make a pencil dot at the center front of the chest pencil line **E** on your doll's torso. *(Fig.1-2)*

    Mark a cloth body with either straight pins or the fabric marker. Mark a leather body with the fabric marker.

22. Measure from the pencil dot at the center front neck edge (**A**) to the pencil dot at the center front chest line (**E**) on your doll's torso. Transfer this measurement onto your doll's strip starting from **A**. Make a large dot at the end of this measurement and mark it as **E**. Indicate this measurement on the right side of your doll's strip as **A-E**=___. *(Fig.1-1)*

23. Draw a 1/2-inch solid line at dot **E** to the right of the line on your doll's strip. Draw a 1/2-inch dotted line 1/4 inch above the solid line at the dot **E**. *(Fig.1-1)*

Why are these two (2) lines at **C**, **H**, and **E**? The 1/2-inch solid lines represent the stitching lines of a garment at the natural waist, drop waist (hip), or empire waist (chest). The 1/2-inch dotted lines represent the cutting lines of the garment pattern. The space between the two lines represents the 1/4-inch seam allowance for the natural, drop, or empire waist. These lines are used when measuring the desired length for a doll's outer or under garments.

If, for instance, you want to make a petticoat with three pin-tucks and a 1-inch (5cm) deep hem, you must calculate how long to cut the fabric. Remember to include the waist seam allowance, three times the depth of each pin-tuck, and the depth of the hem plus a small turn-under. I use 1/8 inch (3mm) for a turn-under. If you wish to add slightly gathered lace to the hem, include the width of the lace in your measurements so the finished length of the petticoat meets the **C-B2** length on your doll's Charlotte's Strip. Just some old-fashioned math here.

24. At the top of one of the doll's shoulders, make a large pencil dot at the center of the neck socket edge. This will be **N**, for the neck. Make another large pencil dot on the top of the shoulder at the center upper armhole socket edge. This will be **S**, for the shoulder. *(Fig.1-2)*

    For a cloth-bodied doll with no shoulder plate, use the stitched shoulder seam as the top of the shoulder and the fabric marker for the dots.

    For a cloth- or leather-bodied doll with a shoulder plate, use your judgment about where the top center of the shoulder plate would be and a pencil for the dots. Often, the shoulder plates of some dolls curve over the tops of the arms. Here, you will need to use your imagination as to where the shoulder stops and where the top of the arm might be.

25. Measure the length of the space between these two dots. Indicate this measurement on the right side of your doll's strip as **N-S**=___. *(Fig.1-1)*

26. Cut five (5) more narrow pieces of paper to fit around the thickest part of one of your doll's upper arms and thighs, and around an elbow, wrist, and knee. Tape them in the place where the pieces of paper overlap. Draw pencil lines around where the bottom of the paper pieces touch the upper arm and thigh only. There is no need to draw lines around the elbow, wrist, or knee. *(Fig.1-2)*

    Use the fabric marker for a cloth or leather body.

27. Carefully cut the strips away from the body, one at a time, and measure them. These are the natural upper arm (**U**), elbow (**L**), wrist (**W**), thigh (**T**), and knee (**K**) measurements of your doll's body. Indicate these measurements on the right side of your doll's strip as **U**=___, **L**=___, **W**=___, **T**=___, and **K**=___. *(Fig.1-1)*

28. Make a pencil mark in the center of the crotch between the doll's legs.

For a cloth- or leather-bodied doll, make a mark where the stitched crotch and inner leg seams meet using the fabric marker. Sometimes, a leather doll's legs are so tightly together that it's hard to get between them but do try to make the mark.

29. Measure from the center front waist down to this mark. This is the front crotch measurement. Measure from the center of the back waistline down to this mark. This is the back crotch measurement. Indicate these two measurements on your doll's strip as **Crotch Front**=___ and **Crotch Back**=___. *(Fig.1-1)*

30. Measure from the drawn pencil line around **C** to the drawn pencil line around **T**. Indicate this measurement on your doll's strip as **C-T**=___. Also, measure from the pencil line around **C** to the middle of one of the doll's knees. Indicate this measurement on your doll's strip as **C-K**=___. *(Fig.1-1)*

31. Measure from the dotted line above the solid line at **E** down to **B1** and **B2** on your doll's strip. Indicate these two measurements on your doll's strip as Dress **E-B1**=___. and Slip **E-B2**=___. *(Fig.1-1)*

32. Measure from the dotted line above the solid line at **C** down to **B1** and **B2** on your doll's strip. Indicate these two measurements on your doll's strip as Dress **C-B1**=___. and Slip **C-B2**=___. *(Fig.1-1)*

33. Measure from the dotted line above the solid line at **H** down to **B1** and **B2** on your doll's strip. Indicate these two measurements on your doll's strip as Dress **H-B1**=___. and Slip **H-B2**=___. *(Fig.1-1)*

It is not necessary to create such a detailed strip for every doll. A doll's Charlotte's Strip should have at least the six basic measurements: **A** to **B1**, **C** to **B1**, **C** to **B2**, Waist **C**, Hips **H**, and Thighs **T**. Every measurement you take from a doll, for whatever outfit planned, should be on that doll's Charlotte's Strip. Even head measurements for a bonnet. Each doll has its own unique strip. There is no universal strip for all dolls.

OK?

Now, let's get to drafting patterns.

Drafting a Pattern

Since I entered the wonderful world of dolls way back in 1983 and began sewing for dolls, I always had trouble altering commercial patterns to fit a doll's body. For instance, not all 8-inch (20cm) doll bodies have the same shape. Some have fat tummies, and some are quite thin. Some have wide shoulders, and some have narrow ones. Some have long torsos, and some have short ones. Some have overly long upper legs. And some have arms so short you wonder why they have arms at all. I found that most commercially made patterns are an average fit and sort of hang on a doll, which I am sure it is not too happy about. Dolls have pride, you know. They want to look nice, "spiffy." So, I experimented with pattern making, designing them to fit the different shaped bodies out there. In doing this, I had to first make basic shapes of the dolls' torsos to make the patterns.

Each doll's body is distinct. Patterns are developed to fit these distinctions. Each pattern starts from a basic shape. For instance, a slip bodice pattern is developed from a shape fitted to a doll's upper torso, front and back. Seam allowances are added to the basic shapes to develop a pattern. The pattern will only fit the body for which it was created.

The following detailed, step-by-step instructions should be clear enough. By the time you have waded through them, you will be an old hand at making well-fitted patterns for your dolls.

First, the basic shapes.

Basic Shapes

To create basic shapes for your doll's body, you'll need a measuring tape, paper towel sheets, a few straight pins, a fabric marker, a pencil, a black pen *(not a permanent marker)*, some tape, and clean paper (printer paper will do nicely).

Why paper towels? I tried using soft tissues, but they tear too easily. You can't make pencil marks on them, and ink wicks, making a huge mess. If you are making a shape on a cloth-bodied doll, you don't want the ink to wick through the paper into the cloth body (thus explaining no permanent markers). Regular paper is too stiff to maneuver into a shape. A piece of paper towel proved to be best. The printer paper is used to trace your shapes and make copies.

The following instructions are for a composition or bisque doll body. Additional instructions for a cloth or leather body will be in *italics*. For your reference only, all pencil marks are represented by red ink. All pen marks are represented by black ink. All marks representing the paper towel pieces are in blue ink. Where I mention taping something in place, just know the tape is there. Drawing in pieces of tape would only clutter the line drawings.

The illustrations (Fig.) are line drawings, designed to clearly explain the steps, which can be challenging to convey with photographs. If they appear out of scale or somewhat unusual, that's intentional. They were created to serve as clear examples of my instructions.

FRONT BODICE BASIC SHAPE

Refer to *Fig.2-1* through *Fig.2-13* as examples while you create your doll's front bodice basic shape.

If your doll's body is made of composition or bisque, the torso should still have pencil lines around the empire, natural waist, and hip lines, which were marked while creating your doll's Charlotte's Strip.

If your doll's body is made of cloth, the torso should still have straight pins and/or marks made with a fabric marker. If your doll's body is made of leather, the torso should still have marks made with a fabric marker. If the fabric marker marks have faded but are still slightly visible, I'd redraw them.

1. Draw a pencil line straight down the center front of the doll's torso from the pencil dot at the center neck edge (**A**) to 1/2 inch (1cm) below the center dot on the penciled hip line (**H**).

   Use the fabric marker for a cloth or leather body.

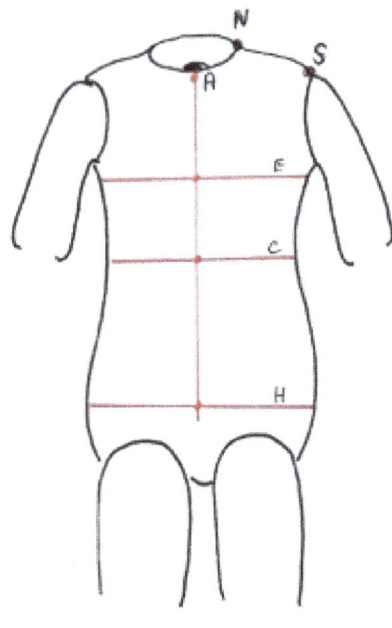

Fig.2-1

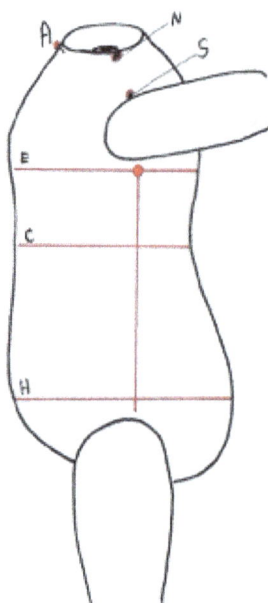

Fig.2-2

2. From the torso's lower armhole socket edge, measure down 3/16 inch (5mm) and make a large pencil dot. From this dot, draw a pencil line down the side of the torso to 1/2 inch below the penciled hip line. *(Fig.2-2)*

For a cloth-bodied doll with sewn-in arms, use a fabric marker. Follow the stitched side seam, making your dot 3/16 inch below where the side/underarm seams meet. Then, draw a line along the torso's side seam to 1/2 inch below the marked hip line.

For a cloth- or leather-bodied doll with the tops of arms tucked under a shoulder plate, use your best judgment to determine where the lower armhole edge might be and use the fabric marker to make your dot. Then, draw a line along the torso's side to 1/2 inch below the marked hip line.

Why the 3/16-inch measurement? The circumference of the torso's arm socket is too small for an armscye. I needed to determine how much deeper an armscye should be to allow a doll's garment to fit nicely over the shoulder/sleeve interface without bunching up. As I mentioned before, dolls want to look nice. I use 3/16-inch seam allowances, so why not add 3/16 inch to the circumference of an armscye? It has proven to be right many times.

3. Draw a pencil line along the top of the shoulder between **N** and **S**. *(Fig.2-3)*

For a cloth-bodied doll with no shoulder plate, use the fabric marker to draw this line along the stitched shoulder seam.

For a cloth- or leather-bodied doll with a shoulder plate, use the pencil to draw this line between the dots you made at N and S.

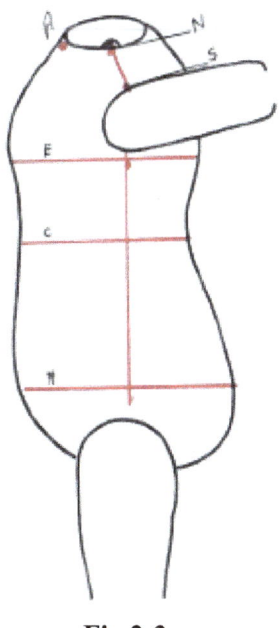

Fig.2-3

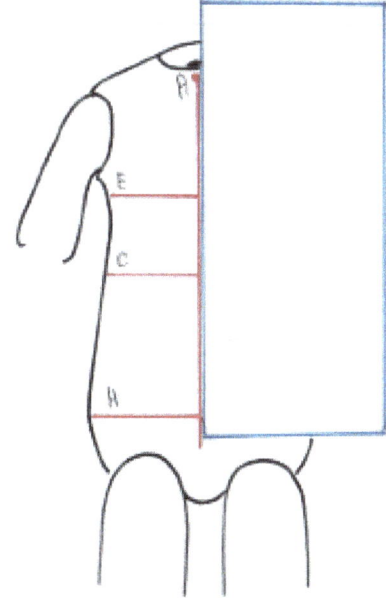

Fig.2-4

4. Measure from 1/2 inch below the penciled hip line **H** to 1 inch (3cm) over the torso's shoulder. Cut a piece of paper towel to this length.

5. Measure from the drawn line along the torso's center front to halfway between the drawn line along the torso's side and center back. Cut the piece of paper towel to this width. Cutting the paper towel these two measurements gives you just enough material to work with.

6. Place a long edge of the paper towel along the drawn line on the torso's center front, taping it in place, with the bottom edge 1/2 inch below **H** and leaving an extension of the paper towel sticking up above the torso's shoulder.

   For cloth- or leather-bodied dolls, follow the same instructions. (Fig.2-4)

7. Carefully fit the paper towel extension around the front and side neck socket edge, creasing the paper towel to fit snugly along the neck socket edge. Draw a broken pencil line along the creased curve on the extension. *(Fig.2-5)*

   For a cloth-bodied doll with no shoulder plate, do your best to fit the paper towel extension snugly around the doll's front and side neck, creasing the paper towel extension to fit.

   For a cloth- or leather-bodied doll with a shoulder plate, fit the paper towel extension snugly around the neck socket edge, creasing the paper towel extension to fit.

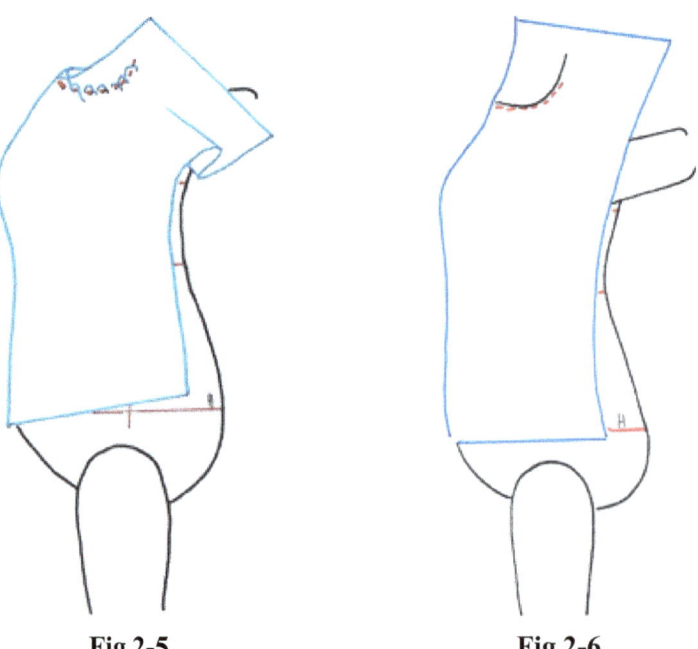

Fig.2-5 **Fig.2-6**

8. Open out the paper towel extension and draw a solid curved pen line over the broken pencil line. *(Fig.2-6)*

9. Trim the excess paper away, cutting along the pen line to create a clean curved edge that fits snugly around the torso's front and side neck socket edge. *(Fig.2-7)*

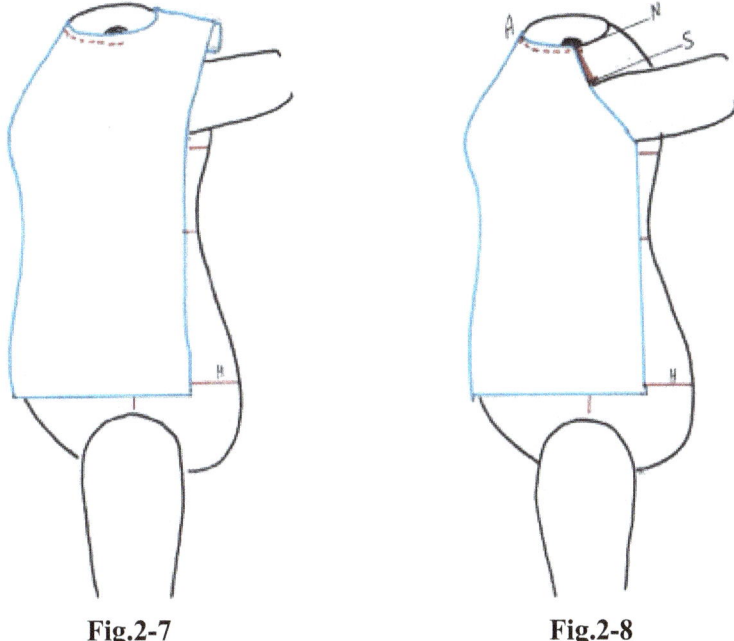

Fig.2-7   Fig.2-8

1. Drape the trimmed paper towel extension smoothly over the shoulder. Fold the extension back along the penciled line on the shoulder. Crease the fold and trim the paper away along the crease. Ensure the trimmed edge aligns with the penciled line on the torso's shoulder. Tape it in place. *(Fig.2-8)*

   For a cloth-bodied doll without a shoulder plate, drape the trimmed paper towel extension smoothly over the shoulder. Fold the extension back along the drawn fabric marker line on the shoulder, creasing the fold. Trim the paper away along the crease, ensuring the trimmed edge is aligned with the drawn line. Tape it in place.

   For a cloth- or leather-bodied doll with a shoulder plate, drape the paper towel extension smoothly over the shoulder. Fold the paper towel extension back over the penciled line on the shoulder, creasing the fold. Trim the paper away along the crease, ensuring the trimmed edge is aligned with the penciled line. Tape it in place.

11. Bend the doll's whole arm backward, shoulder high. Press the paper towel ~~piece~~ around the front edge of the armhole socket, creasing the paper over the edge. Draw a curved broken pencil line over the crease from the shoulder at **S** around to the large pencil dot under the torso's armpit. *(Fig.2-9)*

    *For a cloth-bodied doll with sewn-in attached arms, draw a broken pencil line from **S** and around to the large dot under the armpit, using the front arm/torso seamline as your guide.*

For a cloth- or leather-bodied doll with a shoulder plate, press and crease the paper towel along the front edge of the shoulder plate and around to the large dot under the armpit. Draw a broken pencil line over the crease, using your best judgment for the shape of the front curve. This can be challenging because these dolls often don't have full upper arms.

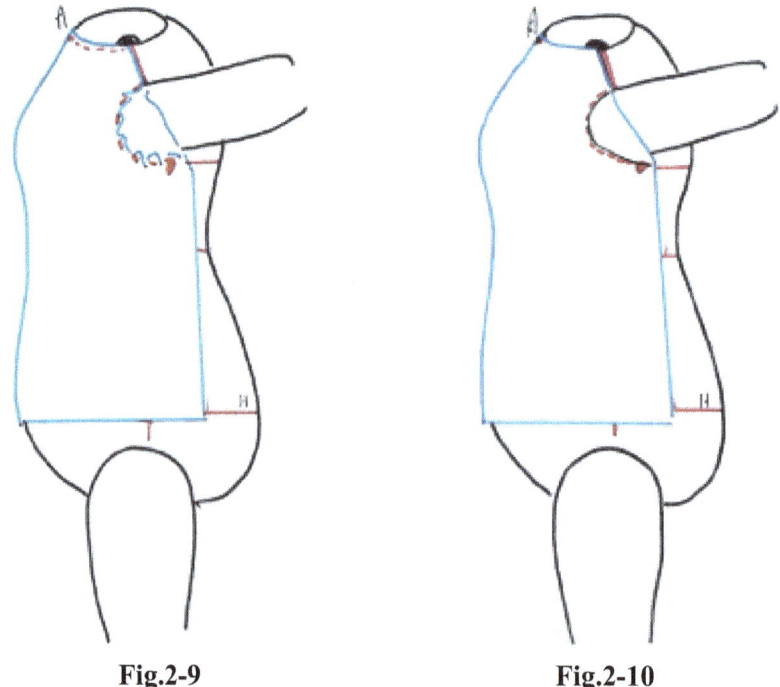

Fig.2-9 Fig.2-10

12. Open the paper towel ~~piece~~ as much as you can. Draw a solid curved pen line over the broken pencil line. *(Fig.2-10)*

13. Trim the excess paper away from the curve, leaving a clean curved edge that fits around the front armhole socket edge from **S** to the large dot under the armpit. Smooth the paper towel over the doll's side. *(Fig.2-11)*

For a cloth-bodied doll with sewn-in attached arms, fit the curve to match the stitched front arm seam around the large dot under the armpit.

*For a cloth- or leather-bodied doll with a shoulder plate, use your judgment for the fit of the trimmed shape of the front curve from **S** to the large dot under the armpit. The arms of these dolls have no real shape, and their tops are tucked under the shoulder plate, making it a bit difficult to decide where to place your mark, but do your best.*

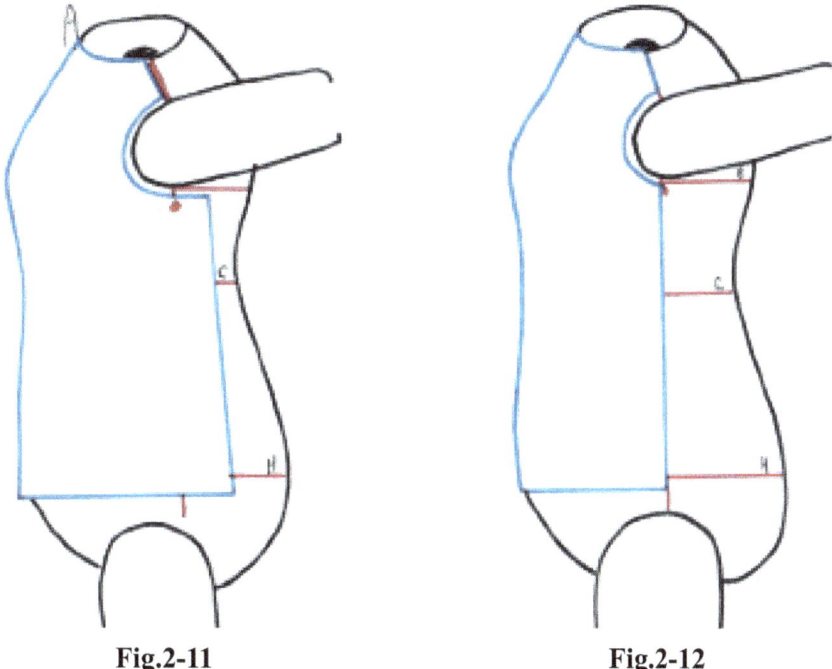

Fig.2-11 **Fig.2-12**

14. Carefully fold the free edge of the paper towel extension along the penciled line on the torso's side. Follow the curve at the waist, creasing the fold. Trim away the excess paper towel piece along the crease, ensuring the trimmed edge is aligned with the penciled line on the torso. Tape it to the torso's side. *(Fig.2-12)*

For a cloth- or leather-bodied doll, follow the same instructions, using the fabric marker line as your guide.

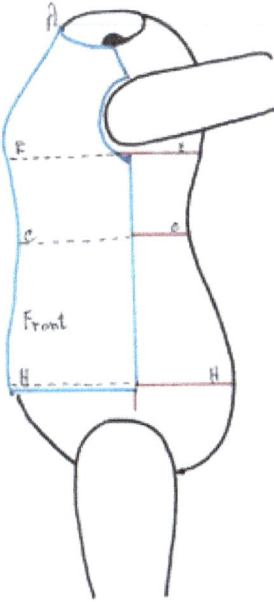

Fig.2-13

15. Using the pencil lines on the torso as a guide, draw broken pen lines across the paper shape at the chest, natural waist, and hip lines. Mark these lines as **E, C,** and **H**. Trim any excess paper towel away along the hip line. Leave the shape taped on the doll. Use the pen to mark this shape as **Front**. *(Fig.2-13)*

For a cloth- or leather-bodied doll, I'd carefully lift the paper shape from the body, temporarily releasing the tape, before drawing the broken lines to prevent any ink from wicking onto the cloth or leather. Re-secure the tape once you've finished drawing the lines.

BACK BODICE BASIC SHAPE

Refer to *Fig.3-1* through *Fig.3-11* as examples while you create your doll's back bodice basic shape.

When creating the back bodice basic shape, ensure you place the piece of paper towel on the side that corresponds with the front bodice basic shape.

1. Make a pencil dot the center back neck edge of your doll's torso. Draw a pencil line straight down the torso's center back from this mark to 1/2 inch below the center dot at **H**. *(Fig.3-1)*

   Use the fabric marker for a cloth or leather body.

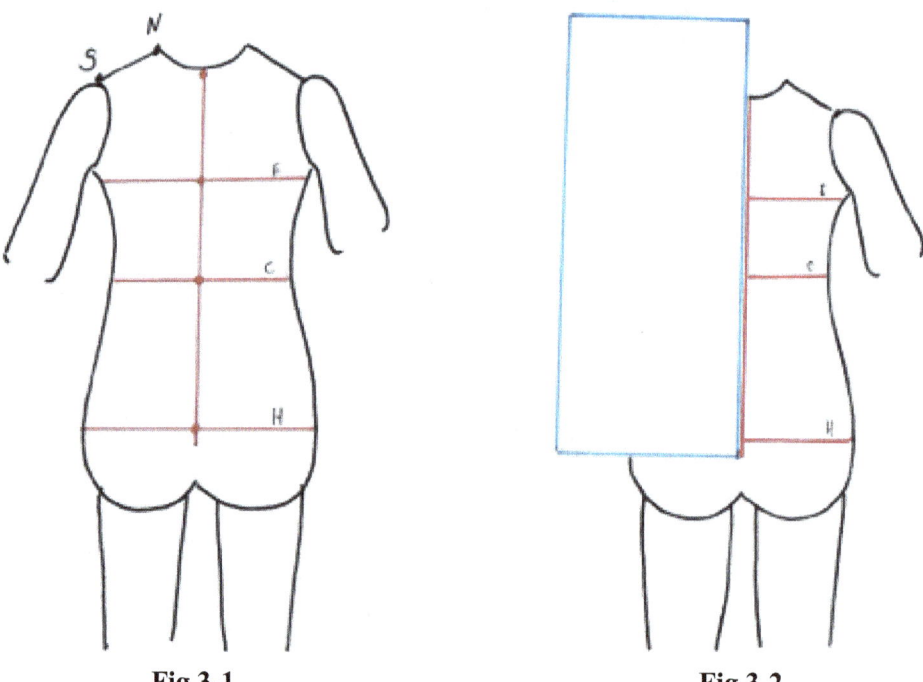

Fig.3-1   Fig.3-2

2. Measure from 1/2 inch below the penciled hip line **H** to 1 inch (3cm) over the torso's shoulder. Cut a piece of paper towel to this length.

3. Measure from the torso's center back to halfway between the drawn line on the torso's side and the drawn line on the center front. Cut the piece of paper towel to this width. By cutting the paper towel according to these two measurements, you will have just enough material to work with.

4. Place a long edge of the paper towel along the drawn line on the torso's center back, taping it in place with the bottom edge 1/2 inch below **H**, leaving an extension of the paper towel sticking up above the torso's shoulder.

   For a cloth- or leather-bodied doll, follow the same instructions.

5. Carefully fit the paper towel extension around the back and side neck socket edge, creasing it to fit snuggly along the neck socket edge. Draw a broken pencil line along the creased curve. *(Fig.3-3)*

   For a cloth-bodied doll with no shoulder plate, do your best to fit the paper towel extension snuggly around the doll's back and side neck, creasing the extension to fit.

   For a cloth- or leather-bodied doll with a shoulder plate, fit the paper towel extension snuggly around the neck socket edge, creasing the extension to fit.

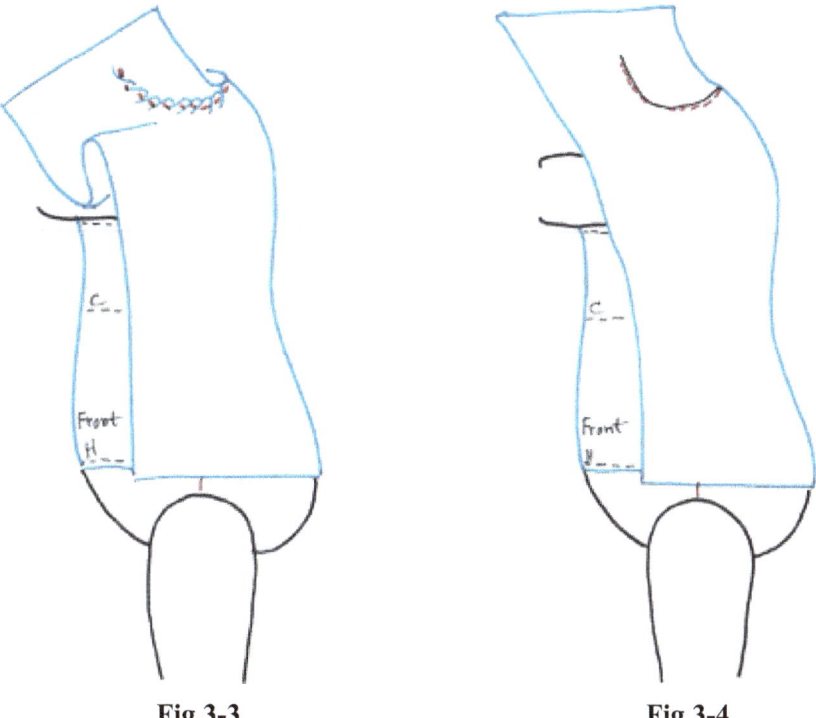

Fig.3-3   **Fig.3-4**

6. Open up the paper towel extension and draw a solid curved pen line over the broken pencil line. *(Fig.3-4)*

7. Trim the excess paper away, cutting along the pen line, making a clean curved edge that fits snugly around the torso's back and side neck socket edge. *(Fig.3-5)*

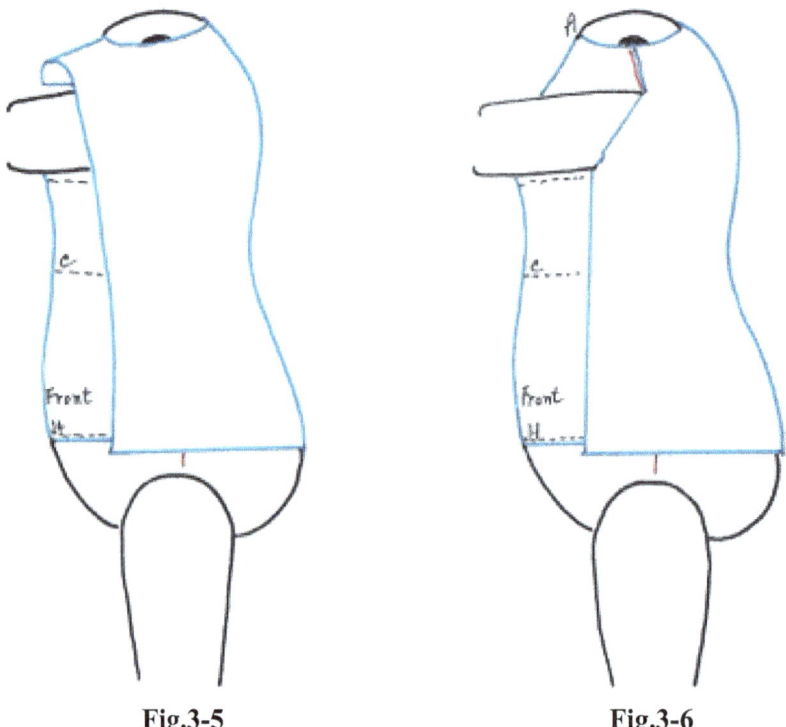

Fig.3-5　　　　　　　　Fig.3-6

8. Drape the trimmed paper towel extension smoothly over the shoulder. Fold the extension back along the penciled line on the shoulder and crease the fold. Trim the paper away along the crease. Ensure the trimmed edge aligns with the penciled line on the torso's shoulder. It should also butt up against the taped bodice front shape shoulder edge. Tape it in place. *(Fig.3-6)*

For a cloth-bodied doll without a shoulder plate, drape the trimmed paper towel extension smoothly over the shoulder. Fold the extension back along the drawn fabric marker line on the shoulder, creasing the fold. Trim the paper away along the crease, ensuring the trimmed edge is aligned with the drawn line. It should also butt up against the taped bodice front shape shoulder edge. Tape it in place.

For a cloth- or leather-bodied doll with a shoulder plate, drape the paper towel extension smoothly over the shoulder. Fold the extension back over the penciled line on the shoulder, creasing the fold. Trim the paper away along the crease, ensuring the trimmed edge is aligned with the penciled line. It should also butt up against the taped bodice front shape shoulder edge. Tape it in place.

9. Bend the doll's arm forward to shoulder height. Press the paper towel around the back edge of the armhole socket, creasing the paper over the edge. Draw a broken curved pencil line over the crease from the shoulder at **S** around to the large pencil dot under the armpit. *(Fig.3-7)*

For a cloth-bodied doll with sewn-in attached arms, draw a broken pencil line from S around to the large dot under the armpit, using the back arm/torso seamline as your guide.

For a cloth- or leather-bodied doll with a shoulder plate, press and crease the paper towel along the back edge of the shoulder plate and around to the large dot under the armpit. Draw a broken pencil line over the crease, using your best judgement as to the shape of the back curve. This can be a challenge because these dolls don't have full upper arms.

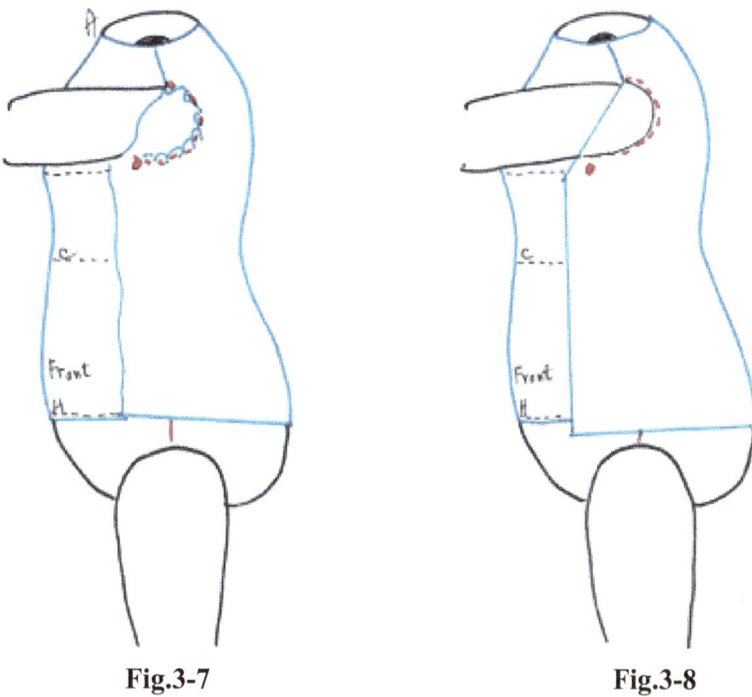

Fig.3-7　　　　　Fig.3-8

10. Open the paper towel as much as you can and draw a solid curved pen line over the broken pencil line. *(Fig.3-8)*

11. Trim the excess paper away from the curve, leaving a clean curved edge that fits around the back armhole socket edge from **S** around to the large pencil dot under the armpit. Smooth the paper towel over the doll's side. *(Fig.3-9)*

For a cloth-bodied doll with sewn-in attached arms, fit the curve to match the stitched back arm seam around the large dot under the armpit.

For a cloth- or leather-bodied doll with a shoulder plate, use your judgment as to the fit of the trimmed shape of the back curve around to the large dot under the armpit.

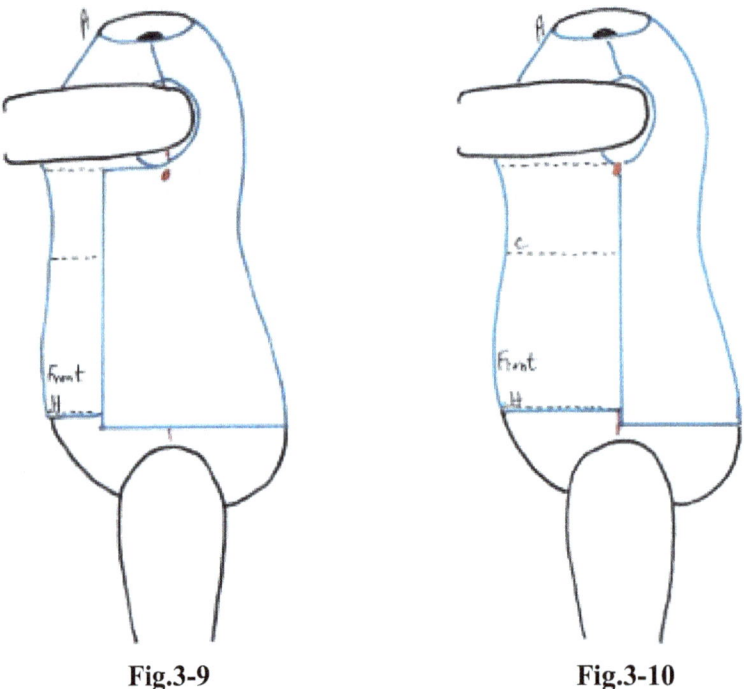

Fig.3-9 **Fig.3-10**

12. Carefully fold the free edge of the paper towel extension over along the penciled line on the torso's side. Follow the curve at the waist, creasing the fold. Trim away the excess paper towel along the crease. Ensure the trimmed edge is aligned with the penciled line on the torso. It should also butt up against the taped bodice front shape side edge. Tape it to the torso's side. *(Fig.3-10)*

For a cloth- or leather-bodied doll follow the same instructions, using the fabric marker line as your guide.

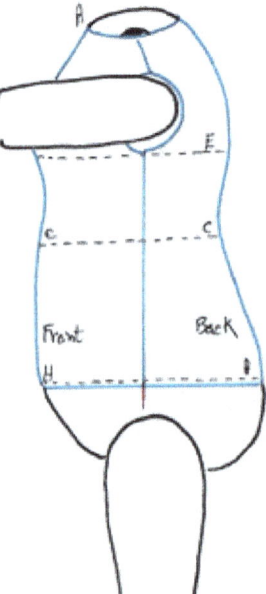

Fig.3-11

13. Using the pencil lines on the torso as a guide, draw broken pen lines across the paper shapes at the chest, natural waist, and hip lines. Mark these lines as **E**, **C**, and **H**. Trim excess paper towel away at **H.** Mark this shape as **Back** with the pen. *(Fig.3-11)*

For a cloth- or leather-bodied doll, carefully lift the paper shape from the body, temporarily releasing the tape, before drawing those broken lines to prevent ink from wicking onto the cloth or leather.

Carefully lift the tape holding the Front and Back bodice basic shapes to your doll's torso and remove both pieces. Cut the tape holding the side and shoulder edges together. Trim away the tape that held the shapes to the torso.

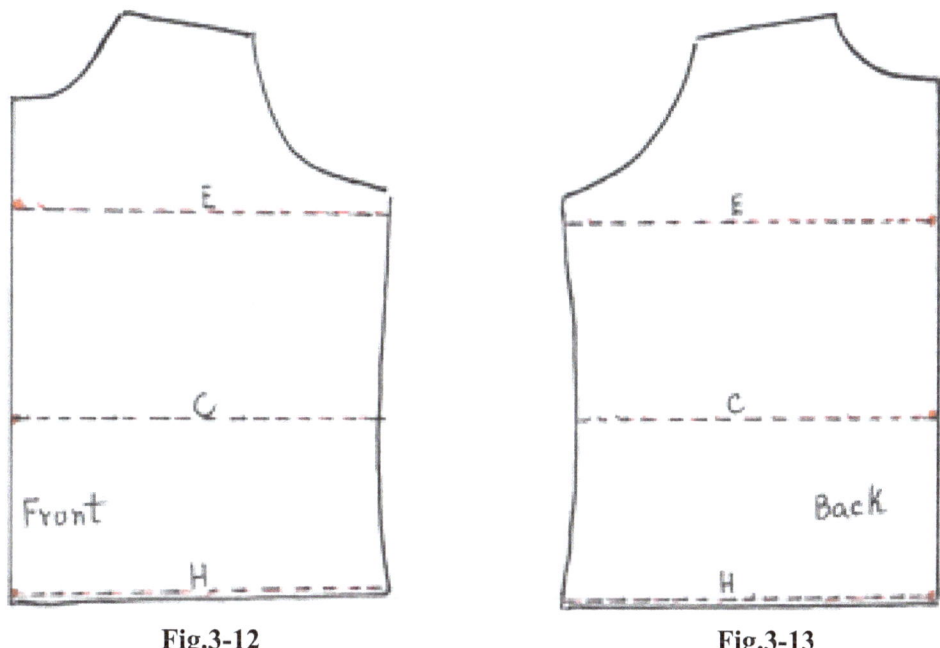

Fig.3-12   Fig.3-13

These drawings *(Fig.3-12 and Fig.3-13)* represent your doll's Front and Back Bodice Basic Shapes. They may not look exactly like the shapes you've made for your doll, but they should be similar.

Copy and cut out three (3) tracings of each of the basic shapes you made for your doll, transferring all marks to the copies. Set them aside for now.

For cloth and leather bodies, follow the same directions.

If your doll's body has more curvature than that of a Bébé doll, you might need to include a dart in the front and back of your basic bodice shapes. Let's do that.

Front Bodice Basic Shape with Dart

Refer to *Fig.4-1* through *Fig.4-4* as examples while creating your doll's front bodice basic shape with a dart.

The darts in the drawings only represent the darts you will be making and will look straight, not showing any curvature of a body.

1. Follow the instructions for the Front Bodice Basic Shape up to where you smoothed the paper towel piece over the doll's side, Step #13, *Fig.2-11.*

2. Allow the free edge of the paper towel piece to fall naturally from under the arm without trying to fit it snugly to the torso. Temporarily tape the paper towel to the body at **H**. *(Fig.4-1)*

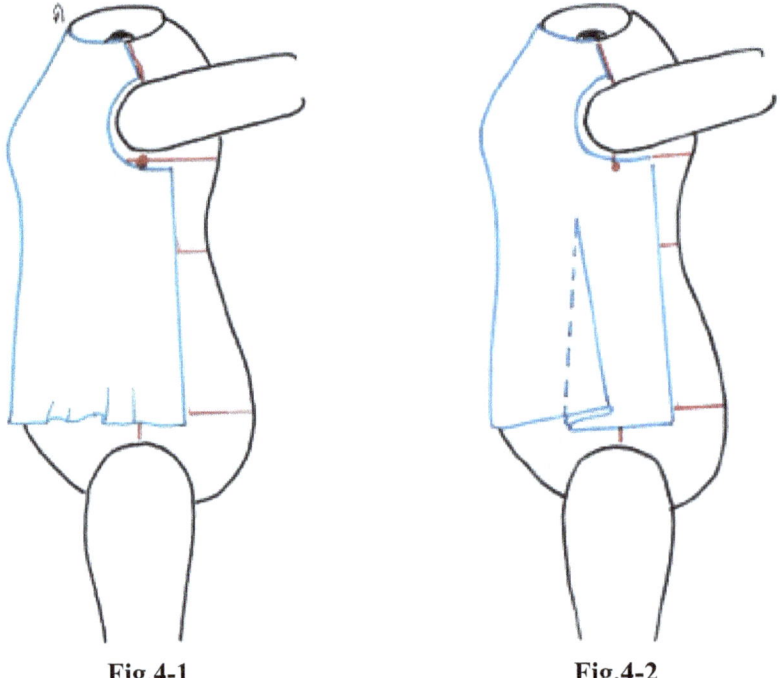

Fig.4-1   Fig.4-2

3. At the hip line, pinch a tuck in the paper towel piece halfway between the center front edge and the torso's side edge, just enough to allow the paper to fit right up against the doll's torso.

4. Crease the tuck, allowing it to fit snugly against the torso. If the tuck is deep and doesn't fit smoothly, clip it at the natural waistline. This will allow the tuck to fit better. Fold the entire tuck over to the torso's side and tape it in place. *(Fig.4-2)*

5. Un-tape the free edge of the paper towel and carefully fold it along the drawn pencil line on the torso's side, creasing the fold. Trim away the excess paper along the crease ensuring the trimmed edge is aligned with the penciled line. Tape it in place. *(Fig.4-3)*

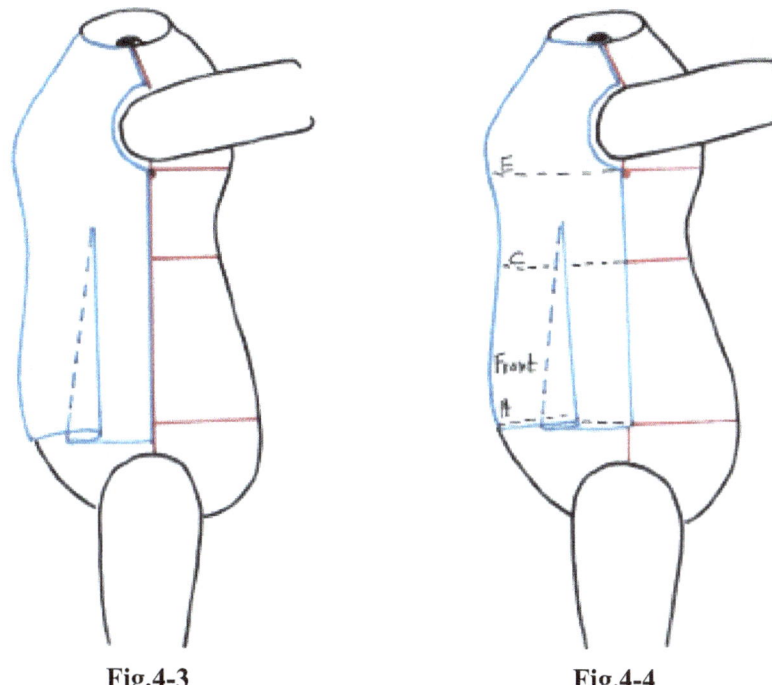

Fig.4-3   **Fig.4-4**

6. Using the pencil lines at the chest, natural waist, and hip lines on your doll's torso as a guide, draw broken pen lines across the paper shapes. Mark these lines as **E**, **C**, and **H**. Trim excess paper towel below the hip line. Mark this shape as **"Front"** with the pen. *(Fig.4-4)*

For a cloth- or leather-bodied doll, carefully lift the paper shape from the body, temporarily releasing the tape, before drawing those broken lines to keep any ink from wicking onto the cloth or leather. Re-set the tape when you're finished drawing the lines.

BACK BODICE BASIC SHAPE WITH DART

Refer to *Fig.5-1* through *Fig.5-4* as examples while creating your doll's back bodice basic shape with a dart.

The darts in the drawings only represent the darts you will be making and will look straight, not showing any curvature of a body.

1. Follow the instructions for the Back Bodice Basic Shape up to where you smoothed the paper towel piece over the doll's side, Step #11, *Fig.3-9*.

2. Allow the free edge of the paper towel piece to fall naturally from under the arm, not trying to fit it snugly to the torso. Temporarily tape the paper towel piece to the body at **H**. *(Fig.5-1)*

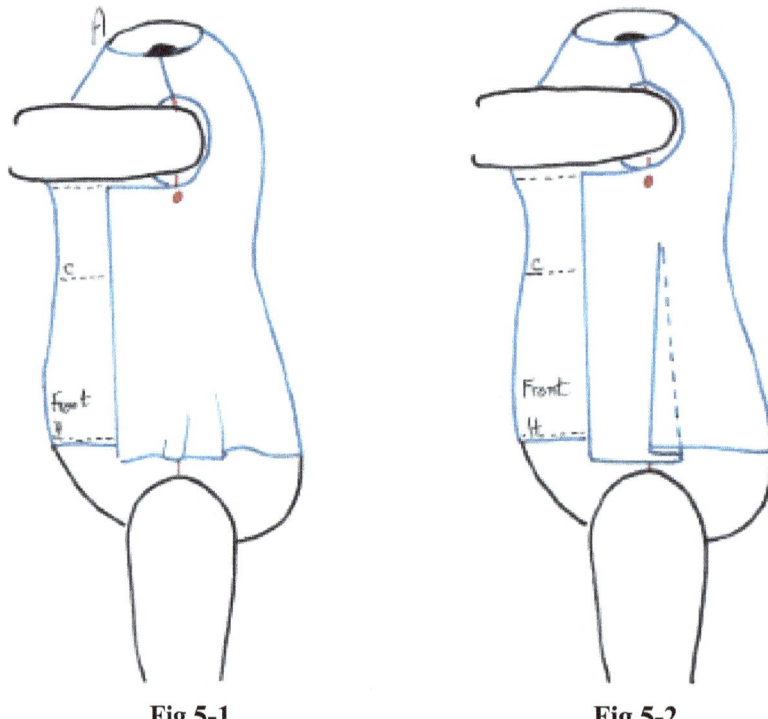

Fig.5-1   **Fig.5-2**

3. At the hip line, pinch a tuck in the paper towel piece half-way between the center back edge and the torso's side edge just enough to allow the paper to fit right up against the doll's torso.

4. Crease the tuck so it fits snugly against the torso. If the tuck is deep and doesn't fit smoothly against the torso, clip it at the natural waist to fit smoothly against the torso. Fold the entire tuck toward the torso's side and tape it in place. *(Fig.5-2)*

5. Un-tape the free edge of the paper towel and carefully fold it over along the drawn pencil line on the torso's side, creasing the fold. Trim away the excess paper along the crease, ensuring the trimmed edge is aligned with the penciled line. It should also butt up against the basic bodice front shape with a dart side edge. Tape it in place. *(Fig.5-3)*

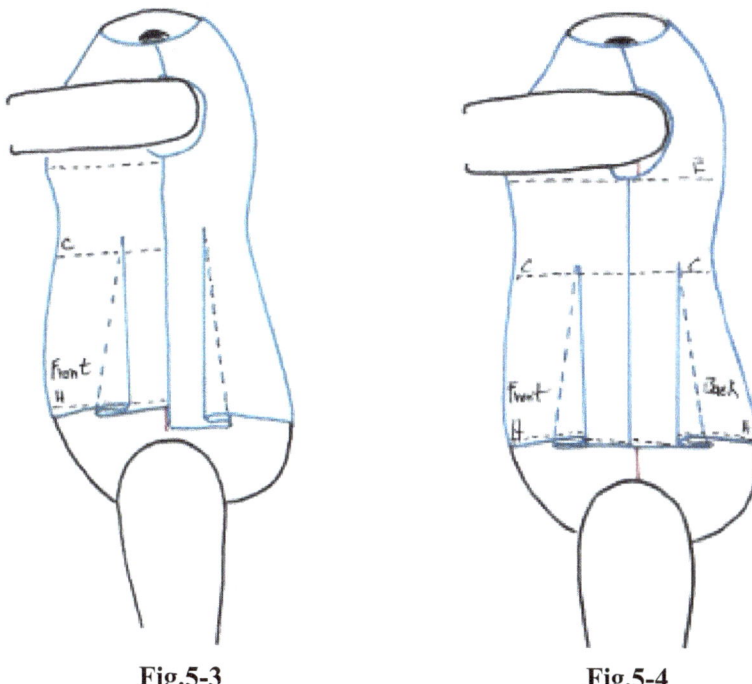

Fig.5-3 **Fig.5-4**

6. Using the pencil lines on your doll's torso as a guide, draw broken pen lines across the paper shapes at the chest, natural waist, and hip lines. Mark these lines as **E**, **C**, and **H**. Trim the excess paper towel at the hip line. Mark this shape as **"Back"** with the pen. *(Fig.5-4)*

For a cloth- or leather-bodied doll, carefully lift the paper shape from the body, temporarily releasing the tape, before drawing broken lines to keep any ink from wicking onto the cloth or leather.

Carefully lift the tape, holding the Front and Back bodice basic shapes to your doll's torso, and remove both pieces. Cut the tape holding the side and shoulder edges together. Trim away the tape pieces that held the shapes to the torso. Carefully cut the tape holding the tucks in place.

When opened, you will see that each tuck (now a dart) has three (3) folds, with or without a clip in the center. Draw short broken pen lines along each fold.

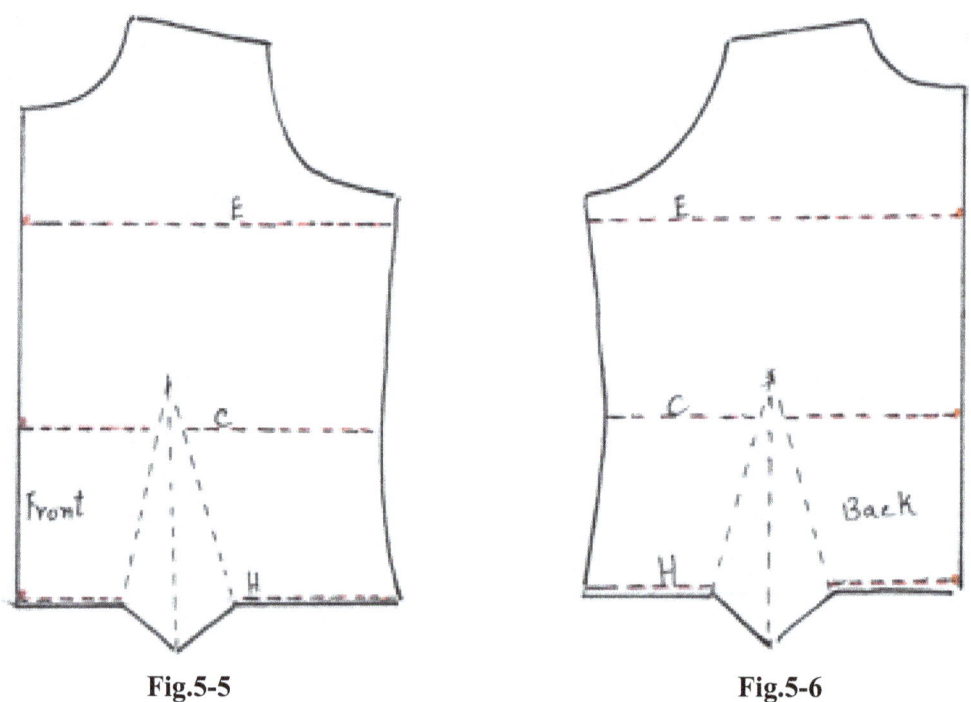

Fig.5-5 **Fig.5-6**

These drawings *(Fig.5-5 and Fig.5-6)* represent your doll's Front and Back Bodice Basic Shapes with Dart. They may not look exactly like the shapes you've made for your doll, but they should could be similar.

Copy and cut out three (3) tracings of each of the basic shapes with darts you made for your doll, transferring all marks to the copies. Set these aside for now.

For cloth and leather bodies, follow the same directions.

SLEEVE BASIC SHAPE
Refer to *Fig.6.1* and *Fig.6-2* as examples while creating your doll's sleeve basic shape. Remember, for your reference only, red ink represents pencil lines/marks.

1. Retape the shoulder edges of the original front and back bodice basic shapes together as they were when first removed from the torso. You'll see why when we move on to developing the sleeve's basic shape.

2. With one of the doll's arms straight down against the body's side and the palm of the hand against the body, measure the length of the outer arm from **S** at the outer shoulder edge, over the upper arm, and down to the doll's wrist **W**. Indicate this measurement on your doll's strip as **S-W=___**.

3. Starting at the shoulder **S**, measure down to the penciled line around the upper arm **U**. Indicate this measurement on your doll's strip as **S-U=___**.

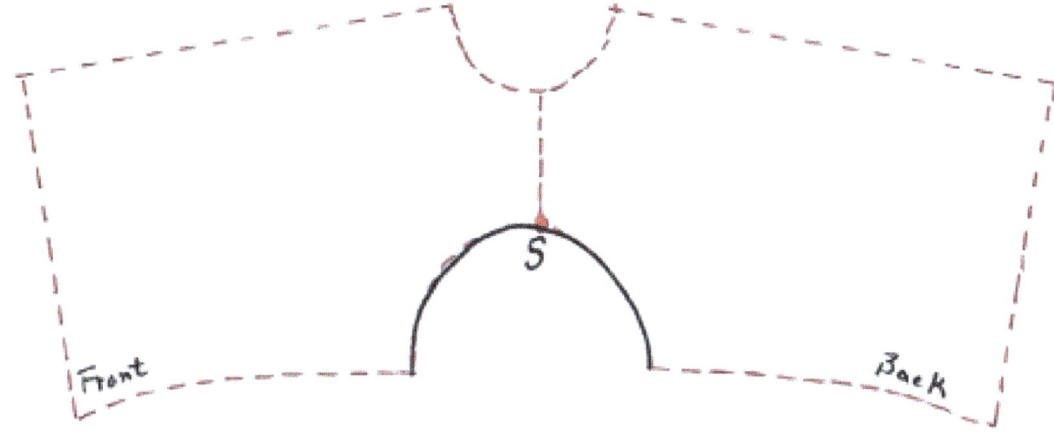

Fig.6-1

4. Place the taped-together shapes (with or without un-taped darts) at the top of a clean piece of paper. Trace the armscye curve onto the paper with the pen, including dot **S**. Trace a light broken outline of the two shapes with the pencil. *(Fig.6-1)*

5. The pencil tracings show the relationship of the armscye to the front and back bodice shapes. They are not intended to be part of the sleeve shape. We are working with the armscye edge only. Set the shapes aside. *(Fig.6-1)*

From your drawing, you can see that the bodice back armscye curve is slightly shallower than the deeper bodice front armscye curve. The helps provide room for forward arm movement, which is not needed in the front, thus avoiding undue stress on the back bodice armscye.

In a sleeve pattern, the back of the sleeve cap is slightly fuller than the front, providing easy forward movement of the doll's arm without placing undue stress on the back of the sleeve cap.

Because of the differences in the front and back armscye curves, and to give the back of the basic sleeve cap the fullness it needs, we will use the front armscye curve for the back of the basic sleeve shape cap, and the back armscye curve for the front of the basic sleeve shape cap. The armscye curve has now become the sleeve shape's Cap.

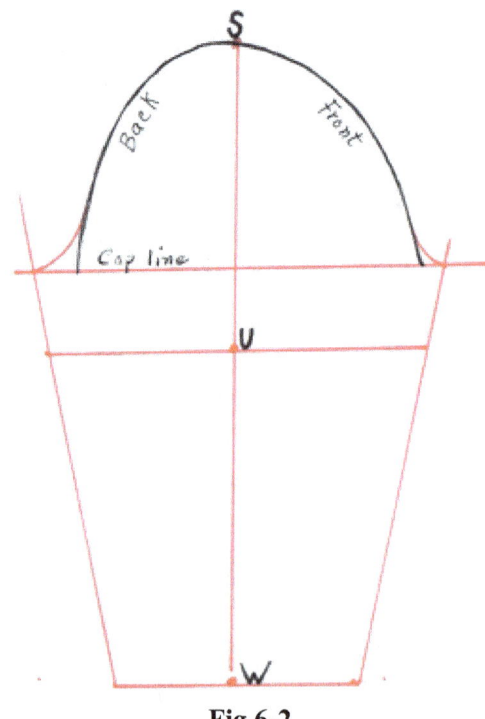

Fig.6-2

6. Draw a horizontal pencil line connecting the two ends of the sleeve cap curve, extending this line beyond each end. This is the Cap line. *(Fig.6-2)*

7. Starting from the dot at **S**, draw a vertical pencil line along the length of the measurement **S-W** on your doll's strip. Make a large pencil dot at the bottom of the line, labeling it **W**. *(Fig.6-2)*

8. Starting from the dot at **S**, transfer the measurement **S-U** (from your doll's strip) to the vertical line. Make a large pencil dot at the end of this measurement, labeling it **U**. *(Fig.6-2)*

9. Using the large dot **U** as the center, raw a horizontal pencil line the length of the measurement **U** (from your doll's strip). *(Fig.6-2)*

10. Using the large dot **W** as the center of this line, draw a horizontal pencil line representing the length of the measurement **W** (from your doll's strip). *(Fig.6-2)*

11. Starting at the ends of line **W**, draw angled pencil lines upward to the ends of line **U**, extending them just past the Cap line. These two slightly angled vertical lines are the basic sleeve shape underarm edges. Connect the sleeve cap curves to the underarm lines with slightly curved lines (little wings). Mark the shape as "Back," "Front," and "S" with the pen. *(Fig.6-2)*

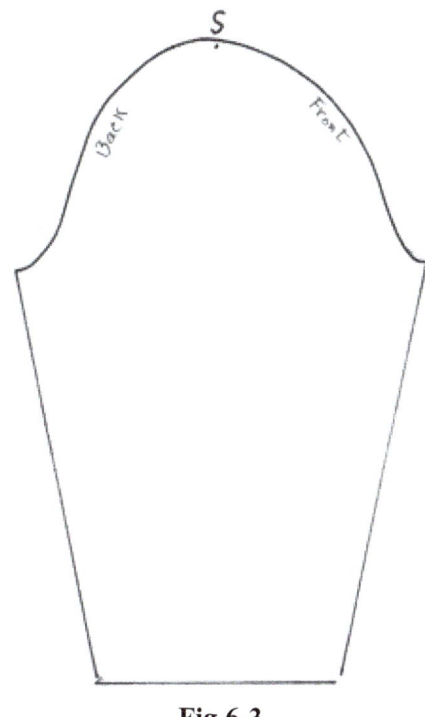

Fig.6-3

This drawing *(Fig.6-3)* represents your doll's Sleeve Basic Shape. It may look awfully skinny for a sleeve but hang in there—it will be used to create a basic sleeve pattern.

Cut out your shape and make two (2) copies, transferring the **S-W**, Cap, and **U** lines, and the dots at **S**, **U,** and **W** to them. Set them aside for now.

DRAWERS BASIC SHAPE

Refer to *Fig.7* as an example while creating your doll's drawers basic shape. Remember, for your reference only, red ink represents pencil lines/marks.

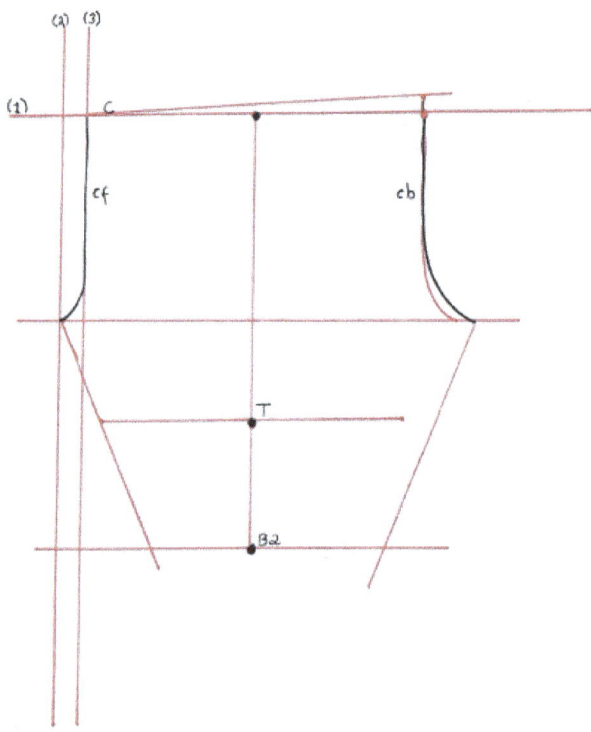

Fig.7-1

1. Draw a horizontal pencil line 2 inches (5cm) from the top and across the width of a clean piece of paper. Label this as line **1**. For now, this line will represent the natural waistline (**C**) of the basic drawers shape.

2. Draw a vertical pencil line 2 inches from the left edge and down the length of the paper. Label this as line **2**.

3. Draw a second vertical pencil line 1/2 inch (1.2cm) to the right of line **2**, down the length of the paper. Label this as line **3**.

   You now have three pencil lines: one horizontal and two vertical. Right? *(Fig.7-1)*

4. Locate the Front Crotch measurement on your doll's strip. Draw this measurement onto line **3** with the pencil, starting at waistline (**C**) and ending with a slight curve to the left, making a **J**-shaped line. *(Fig.7-1)*

   See it? Good.

5. Cut the paper away along the **J**-shaped line to the top of the paper. The cut edge, from **C** downward to the end of the curved **J** edge, is the center front edge of the drawer's basic shape. Mark it as **cf**. *(Fig.7-1)*

6. From the top of **cf** at **C** and along line **1**, measure half the natural waistline measurement (**C** on your doll's strip) and make a large pencil dot. *(Fig.7-1)*

7. Fold the center front edge over to this dot, matching the line **1** with **C**. Trace the center front edge with the pencil, creating a backward **J**-shaped line. OK so far? This is the center back edge of the drawer's basic shape. Mark it as **cb**. *(Fig.7-1)*

    From your doll's strip, you can see that the Crotch Back measurement is slightly longer than the Crotch Front. Therefore, we must make the curve of the backward **J**-shaped line a bit longer and shallower.

8. Draw the crotch back measurement over the pencil line of the center back edge with the pen, starting at waistline **C**, ending with a shallow, slightly longer curve to the right. Using *Fig. 7-1* as your guide, make this curve shallower and longer than the front crotch curve.

9. Draw a horizontal pencil line through the bottom ends of the center front and center back crotch curves. *(Fig.7-1)*

10. Make a large pen dot at the center of waistline **C**. *(Fig.7-1)*

11. Using the measurement **C-B2** (from your doll's strip), and starting from this large pen dot, draw a vertical pencil line from **C** to **B2**. Make a large pen dot at the end of this measurement, labeling it **B2**. *(Fig.7-1)*

12. Draw a horizontal pencil line through **B2** across the paper. This line represents the drawer's finished hemline and should be horizontal to the edge of the paper. *(Fig.7-1)*

13. Using the measurement **C-T** (from your doll's strip), and starting from the large pen dot at **C**, transfer this measurement along the vertical **C-B2** line, making a large pen dot at the end, labeling it **T**. *(Fig.7-1)*

14. Using the large pen dot **T** as the center, draw a horizontal pencil line to the length of measurement **T** (from your doll's strip).

15. Draw a pencil line from the end of the center front crotch curve downward through the end of the line at **T**, continuing downward to line **B2**. This is the drawer's front inner leg line. *(Fig.7-1)*

16. Cut the paper away from and along the front inner leg line. Fold the cut edge over, matching the ends of the front and back crotch curves. With the pencil, trace the front inner leg line down to line **B2**, creating a matching back inner leg line. *(Fig.7-1)*

Now, do you see a drawer's basic shape forming here? To accommodate a doll's backside, the back of the drawers will need just a tad more length from the back waistline to the crotch.

17. Extend the top of the center back line 1/2 inch (1cm) upward. Draw a new penciled waistline **C** from the top of the center front line to the new top of the center back line. *(Fig.7-1)*

This added 1/2 inch length to the back of the drawers is suitable for most dolls. Larger dolls may need an additional 3/4 inch (2cm) to 1 inch (3cm). Smaller dolls may need only 1/4 inch (6mm) of additional length.

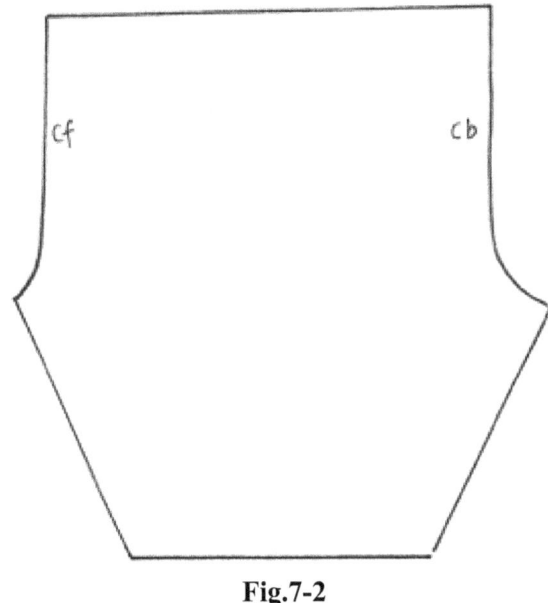

Fig.7-2

This drawing *(Fig.7-2)* represents your doll's Drawers Basic Shape. It, like the sleeve's basic shape, looks very skinny and couldn't possibly be used for a pattern. It's not meant to. It will be used to make a drawer's basic pattern.

Cut out and trace two (2) copies of the basic drawer's shape you made for your doll, transferring **cf** and **cb**, the **C-B2** line, and the dots (**C, T,** and **B2**) to the copies. Set them aside for now.

You might be looking at all the basic shapes you've made for your doll so far and thinking that they look a bit strange. They really do. You might also be wondering how they can be developed into patterns? That's OK. Follow along with me, and I'll show you how these shapes are developed into some basic patterns.

Basic Patterns

The following instructions explain how to use your basic shapes to draft patterns for a doll's pair of drawers, drop-waist slip bodice, drop-waist dress bodice, and sleeve. In the line drawings, you will see little arrows inside a seam allowance. These are for your reference only, showing the direction of added or deleted width or length to a basic shape. Also, for your reference only, **red** ink lines/marks/arrows represent pencil lines/marks/darts. You will need clean pieces of paper, a clear ruler, a pencil, and a black pen.

For your reference only, while developing the Slip and Dress Bodice Basic Patterns, I kept the pencil-traced outline of the original Basic Shapes in all the drawings so you can see how the basic shapes are gradually, step-by-step, developed into patterns. For the development of the Sleeves and Drawers basic patterns, keeping the outline of the original basic shapes for comparison was not necessary.

Drawers

Drawers Basic Pattern

Refer to *Fig.8-1* through *Fig.8-3* as examples for drafting your doll's drawer's basic pattern using your drawer's basic shape.

1. Draw a pencil line 1 inch (3cm) above and across the bottom edge of a clean piece of paper. Ensure the piece of paper is large enough to make a pattern for your doll.

   Drawers should fit loosely. The thigh measurement is the most important in drafting a drawers pattern. When placing a pair of drawers on a doll, you have to get past the thighs before you can get the drawers over the doll's hips and up to the waist.

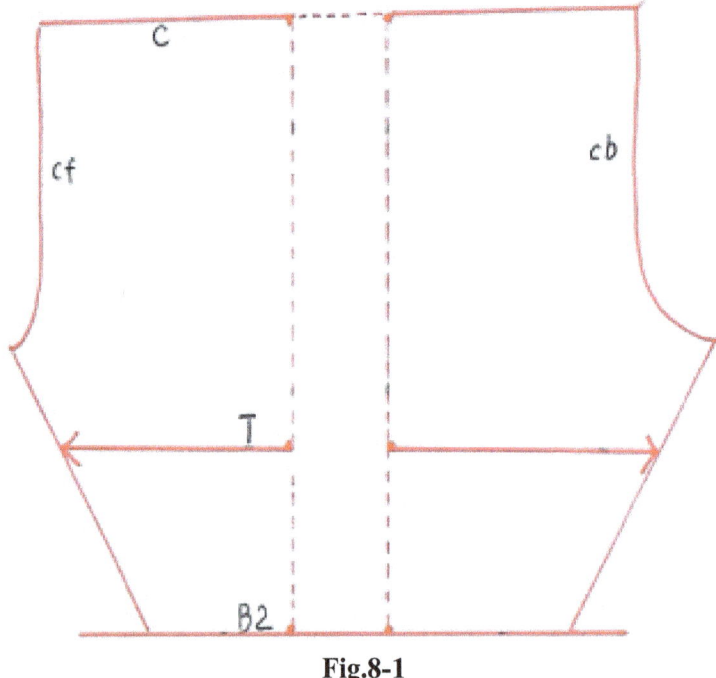

Fig.8-1

2. Fold the shape in half, matching the two inner leg edges. Cut the shape in half along the fold. Place the **B2** edge of the two halves on the drawn line. *(Fig.8-1)*

3. Spread the halves wide enough apart to accommodate the **T** measurement from your doll's strip. Add a slight additional width (your decision) to give the drawers some "wiggle room" around the doll's thighs. The **T** measurement plus your additional width will be from the front inner leg edge to the back inner leg edge at the **T** level (arrows), not within the added space between the two halves. *(Fig.8-1)*

4. Trace a solid pencil line around the shape you've just made, joining the two halves together. Set this aside. This is the start of your drawer's basic pattern. *(Fig.8-2)*

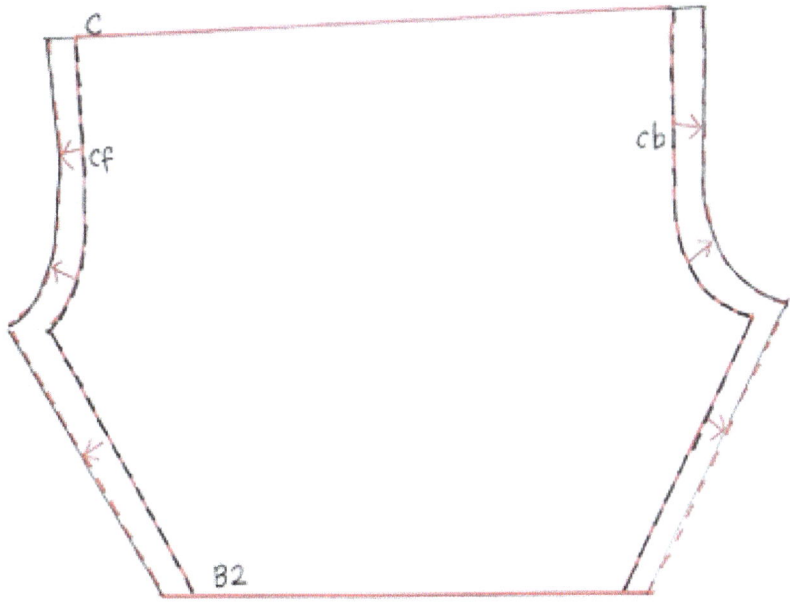
Fig.8-2

5. Measure 3/16 inch (5mm) outside the **cf**, **cb**, and inner leg edges, making little pencil marks at each measurement. Draw solid pen lines over these marks and broken pen lines over the original pencil tracing. You have added 3/16-inch seam allowances outside the basic shape. *(Fig.8-2)*

6. Mark the shape's front edge as **cf** (center front) and the back edge as **cb** (center back) with the pen, both next to the broken lines. *(Fig.8-2)*

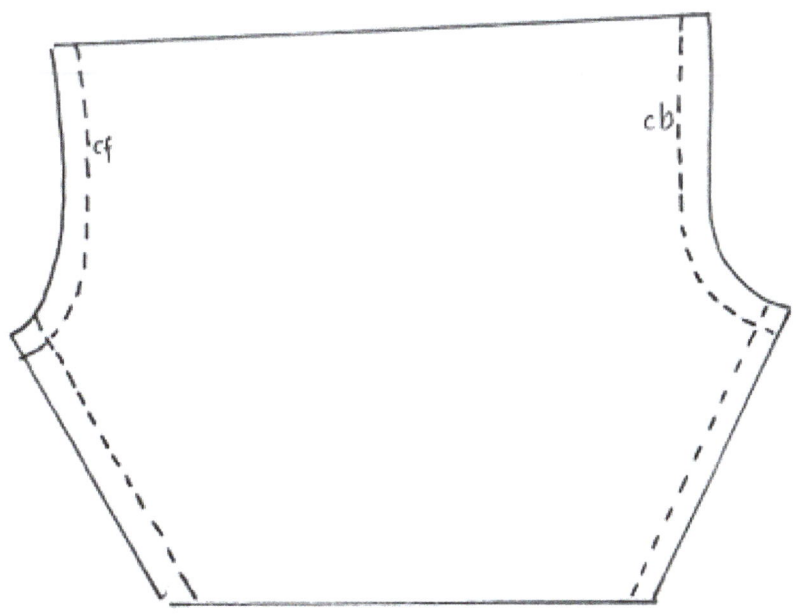
Fig.8-3

This drawing *(Fig.8-3)* represents your doll's Drawers Basic Pattern.

Do nothing with the **B2** edge. When it comes to having a pair of drawers with a hem and/or pintucks or adding lace insertion or lace edging, you consider these when cutting your fabric. You want the finished length to match your basic pattern length.

Cut out the Drawers Basic Pattern you made for your doll and make two copies, marking the copies with the seam allowances, **cf**, **cb**, **C**, and **B2**.

The following are instructions for adding length to the drawer's waist edge (**C**) for either a drawstring casing or a waistband.

DRAWSTRING WAIST CASING

So far, you've drafted your drawer's basic pattern up to adding seam allowances to the front, back, and inner leg edges in Step #5, *Fig.8-2.* The following instructions are for adding a 1/4-inch (6mm) wide drawstring casing, which is average for dolls standing between 10 inches (25cm) and 20 inches (51cm) tall. Taller dolls might need a wider casing. Smaller dolls might need a casing as narrow as 3/16 inch (5mm).

Refer to *Fig.8-4* as an example for drafting your doll's drawers with a drawstring waist basic pattern using your drawer's basic pattern.

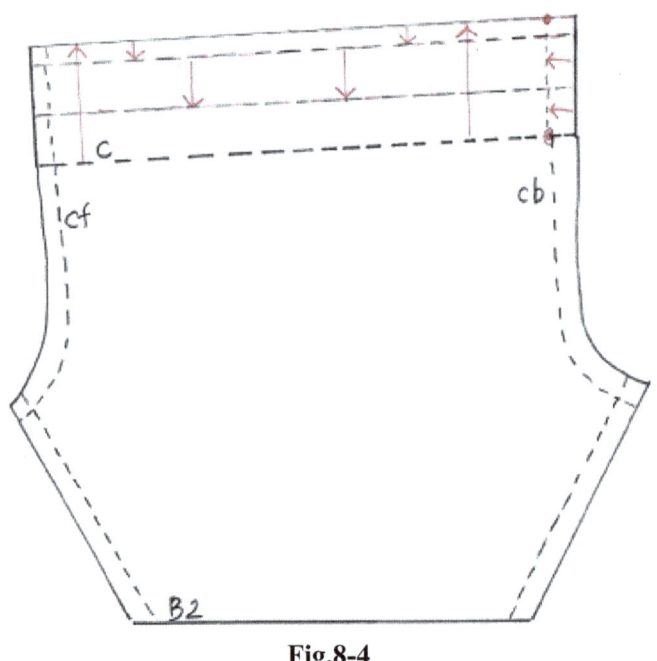

Fig.8-4

1. Trace a solid pen line around your doll's Drawers Basic Pattern onto a clean piece of paper, with a broken line across **C**. Leave enough space above the broken **C** line to work with. Add markings **cf** and **cb** and seam allowances to this tracing.

2. Measure 7/8 inch (2cm) upward from and along the broken line at **C**, making little pencil marks at each measurement. Extend the **cf** and **cb** edges up to these marks. Draw a solid pen line over the pencil marks, connecting the extended **cf** and **cb** lines. *(Fig.8-4)*

3. Measure 1/8 inch (3mm) downward from and along this solid pen line, making little pencil marks at each measurement. Draw a broken pen line over these marks.

4. Measure 1/2 inch (1cm) downward from and along this broken pen line, making little pencil marks at each measurement. Draw a broken pen line over these marks. These two broken lines are the fold lines for the 1/4-inch drawstring casing. *(Fig.8-4)*

5. At the back edge of the shape, and the waist **C** line, measure 3/16 inch inward and make a large pencil dot. Then, at the back edge of the 7/8-inch solid line, measure 3/16 inch inward and make a large pencil dot. Draw a broken pen line connecting these two large pencil dots. This short broken line is the fold line for the back entrance for a drawstring into the casing. *(Fig.8-4)*

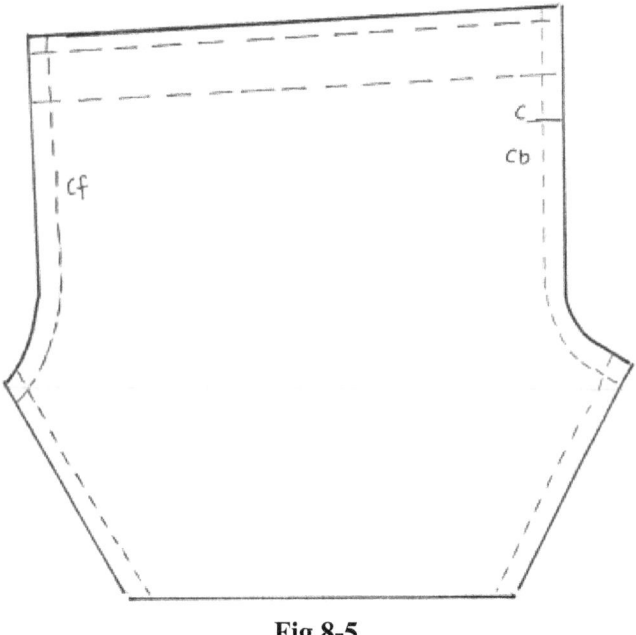

Fig.8-5

This drawing *(Fig.8-5)* represents your doll's Drawers with a Drawstring Waist Basic Pattern.

Cut out the Drawers with a Drawstring Waist Basic Pattern you made for your doll and have fun making a pair. If you want pin-tucks and a lace edge, make the pin-tucks and sew the lace to the edge of a piece of fabric before cutting out your drawers pattern.

Waistband-Waist

So far, you have created the drawers basic pattern until where we add seam allowances to the front, back, and inner leg edges, Step #5, *Fig.8-2*. The following instructions are for adding a waist seam allowance for attaching a waistband to the drawers.

Refer to *Fig.8-6* as an example for drafting your doll's drawers with a waistband-waist basic pattern using your drawers basic pattern.

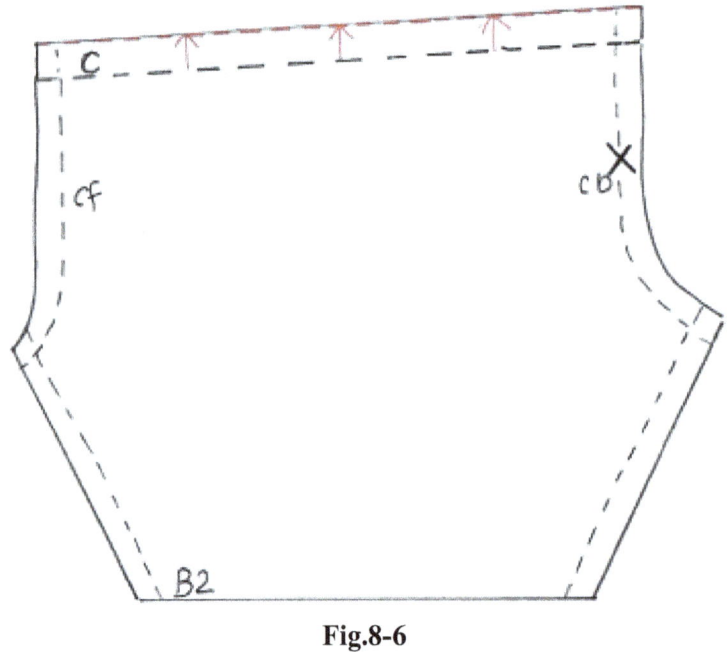

Fig.8-6

1. Trace a solid pen line around your doll's Drawers Basic Pattern onto a clean piece of paper, with a broken line across **C**. Add markings **cf** and **cb** and seam allowances to this tracing. *(Fig.8-6)*

2. Measure 1/4 inch (6mm) upward from and along the broken pen marks along **C**, making little pencil marks at each measurement. Extend the front and back edges up to these marks. Draw a solid pen line over the pencil marks, connecting the extended front and back edges. You are adding a 1/4-inch waist seam allowance to the drawer's waist edge. *(Fig.8-6)*

3. From the back end of the waistline, measure 2 inches (5cm) downward and make a large **X** on the back seam allowance stitching line. The back seam will be sewn from the crotch to this **X**, leaving a placket opening from **X** to the top of **cb**. *(Fig.8-6)*

A placket creates a finished edge for a placket opening. For a placket, you will need a piece of fabric twice as long as the placket opening and wide enough to make a 1/4-inch wide placket plus a 3/16-inch (3mm) seam allowance along each long edge.

A waistband needs the measurement around **C**, as well some leeway for a 3/16-inch seam allowance at each end. This should be to ensure that the ends of the finished waistband overlap by 1/4 inch.

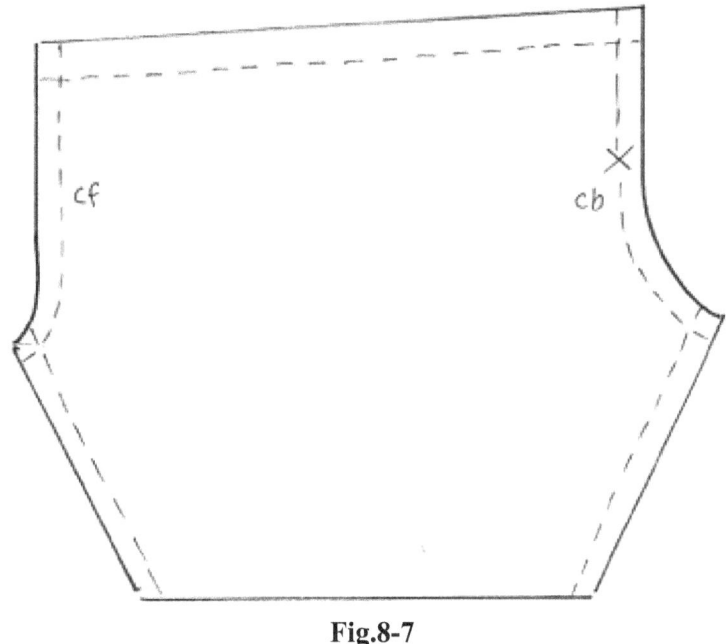

Fig.8-7

This drawing *(Fig.8-7)* represents your doll's Drawers with a Waistband-Waist Basic Pattern.

Cut out the Drawers with a Waistband-Waist Basic Pattern you made for your doll and have fun making a pair. If you want pin-tucks and a lace edge, make the pin-tucks and sew the lace to the edge of a piece of fabric before cutting out your drawers pattern.

"Alright," you say, "Now, how do I make a hem in my doll's drawers?"

HEM

Refer to *Fig.8-8* as an example of creating your doll's drawers with a hem basic pattern using your drawers basic pattern with a waistband-waist.

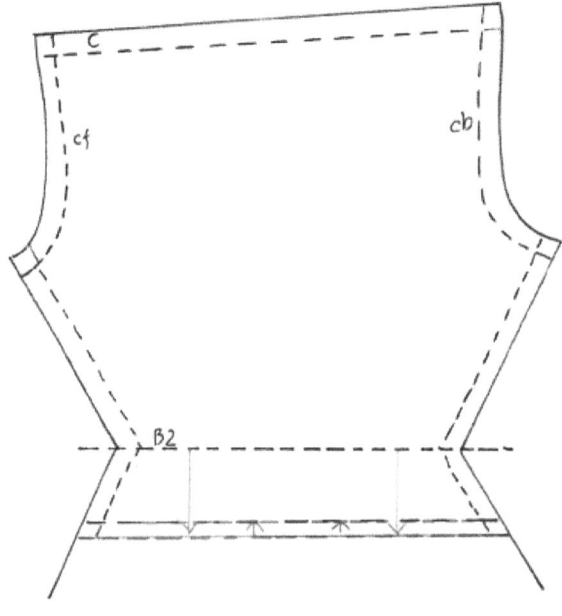

Fig.8-8

1. Draw a broken pen line on a clean piece of paper about 3 inches (8cm) above the bottom edge. Ensure the paper is large enough to accommodate your doll's drawers basic pattern with either the drawstring-waist or waistband-waist. Place the **B2** end of the pattern on the broken line and trace a solid pen line around the pattern. Add markings on the pattern to the tracing. *(Fig.8-8)*

2. Turn the pattern upside down and place it against the drawn broken line of the traced pattern. Trace a solid pen line of just the inner leg edges down to the edge of the paper. *(Fig.8-8)*

3. Decide how deep a hem you want and add 1/8 inch (3mm). Using your hem measurement plus the 1/8 inch, measure downward from and along the drawn broken line, making little pencil marks at each measurement. Draw a solid pen line through the pencil marks. *(Fig.8-8)*

4. Measure 1/8 inch upward from and along this solid line, making little pencil marks at each measurement. Draw a broken pen line through the pencil marks. Draw the 3/16-inch (5mm) seam allowance in each inner leg edge. The drawn broken pen line along **B2** is now the hem fold-up line. *(Fig.8-8)*

You have added a hem plus a 1/8-inch turn-over to the bottom edge of your doll's drawers basic pattern. The hem will fit nicely inside the bottom edge with no puckers. If you just added length to the pattern as it is, you would have trouble fitting the hem inside the bottom edge, resulting in major puckers in the outside of the hem.

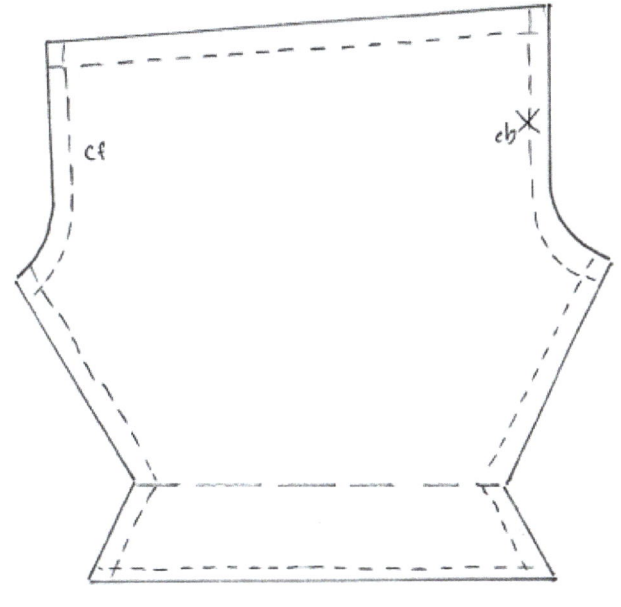

Fig.8-9

This drawing *(Fig.8-9)* represents your doll's Drawers with a Hem Basic Pattern.

Cut out the Drawers with a Hem you made for your doll and have fun making a pair. If you want pin-tucks, I'd make them in a piece of fabric before cutting out the drawers pattern.

Slip

Drop-Waist Bodice Basic Pattern
Refer to *Fig.9-1* through *Fig.9-9* as examples for drafting your doll's front and back slip drop-waist bodice basic patterns using your bodice basic shapes.
Instructions for a natural-waist or empire-waist front and back slip bodice basic patterns are the same, except you start with either **C** or **E** on the drawn line. You will need some clean paper, a ruler, a pencil, and a black pen. Remember, for your reference only, the little arrows indicate direction and red ink represents pencil lines/marks/arrows.

1. Draw a pencil line 2 inches (5cm) up from and across the bottom edge of a clean piece of paper.

2. Place the hip edges **H** of one set of the front and back slip drop-waist bodice basic shapes on the line, about 3 inches (8cm) apart and facing away from each other. Trace a solid pencil line around each basic shape. Set the shapes aside. *(Fig.9-1 and Fig.9-2)*

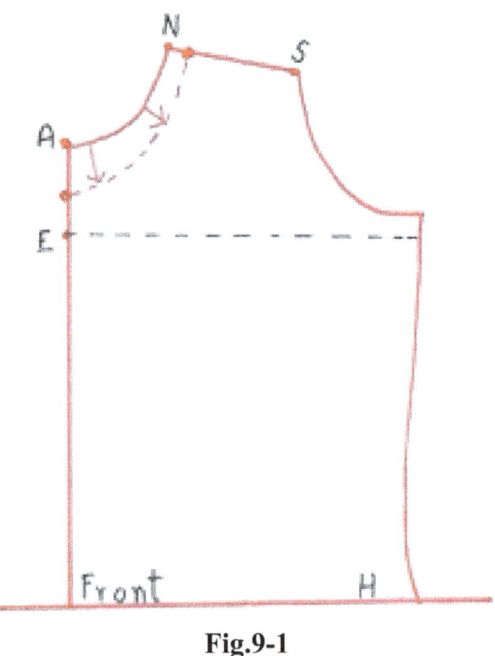
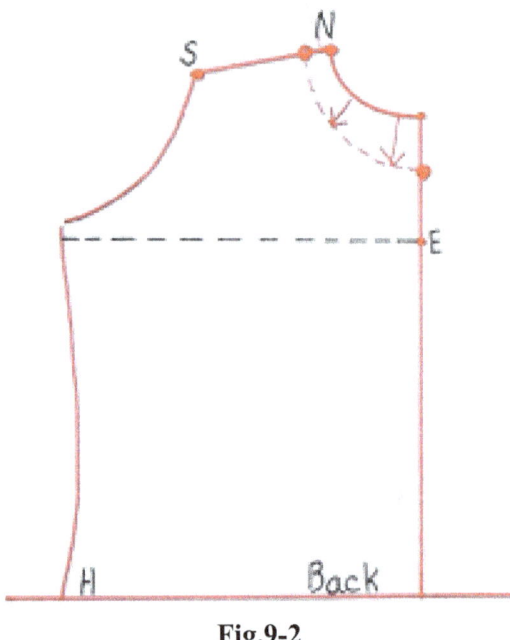

Fig.9-1 Fig.9-2

3. Because the necklines of the front and back of a slip are not usually so high up around the neck, adjustments to the neck edges of the front and back shapes are needed. Find the measurement **A-E** on your doll's strip. You will be using half of this for the adjustments.

4. Transfer this measurement, half of **A-E**, to the front and back shapes, starting from **A** in the front and from the center back neck edge in the back, making a large pencil dot at the end of these measurements. *(Fig.9-1 and Fig.9-2)*

   Why do I use half of **A-E** and **3/16** inch (5mm) as numbers to reduce the neck edges of these shapes for a slip bodice? In all my years of making patterns for dolls and experimenting with various measurements, these two became standard. Finished slip bodices always appeared to fit right. If you wish to use different numbers, that is OK. It's the method of reducing the neck and armscye edges of basic bodice shapes for slip bodices that is important here.

5. Because the neck edge **N** of the shoulder **N-S** is also too close around the neck, adjustments to the shoulder edges of both the front and back shapes are needed here. From **N**, measure 3/16 inch along each shoulder edge and make a large pencil dot. *(Fig.9-1 and Fig.9-2)*

6. Draw a broken pencil line from the pencil dots on the shoulder edges down to the large pencil dots on the front and back edges, following the curves of the original pen tracings as much as possible. These are the new slip basic pattern front and back neck edges. *(Fig.9-1 and Fig.9-2)*

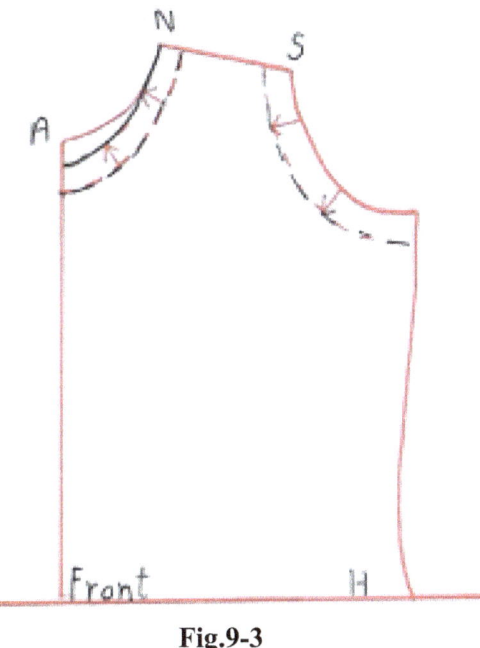

Fig.9-3 **Fig.9-4**

7. Measure 3/16 inch upward from and along each of the new neck edges, making little pencil marks at each measurement. Draw solid pen lines over the pencil marks and broken pen lines over the broken pencil lines of the new necklines. You are adding 3/16-inch seam allowances to each neck edge. *(Fig.9-3 and Fig.9-4)*

8. Measure 3/16 inch inward from and along the traced armscye edge of both the front and back shapes, making little pencil marks at each measurement. Draw broken pen lines over these marks and solid pen lines over the original pencil tracings. You are adding 3/16-inch seam allowances inside each armscye edge. *(Fig.9-3 and Fig.9-4)*

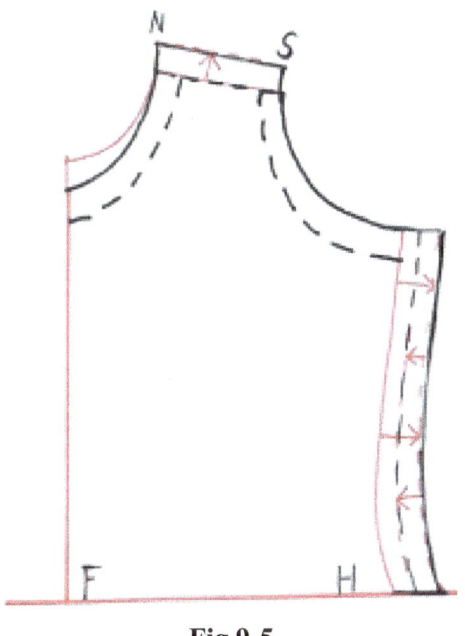 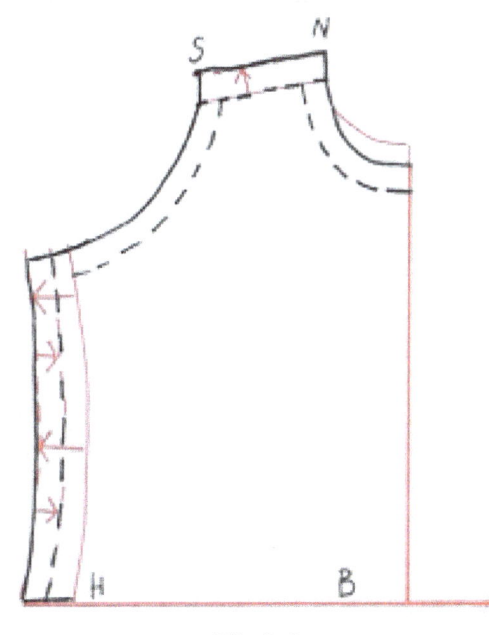

Fig.9-5 **Fig.9-6**

9. Measure 3/16 inch upward from and along the shoulder edges of both the front and back shapes, making little pencil marks at each measurement. Draw solid pen lines over these marks and broken pen lines over the original pencil tracings. You are adding 3/16-inch seam allowances to each shoulder edge. *(Fig.9-5 and Fig.9-6)*

   Along with adding seam allowances to the side edges of the bodice front and back basic shapes, a little more width ("wiggle room" all around the torso) is needed, or the slip drop-waist bodice basic pattern developed from these shapes will be too tight. After years of sewing for dolls, I decided that a 1-inch (3cm) addition all around was just enough.

10. Measure 7/16 inch (1cm) outward along the side edges of both the front and back shapes, making little pencil marks at each measurement. Extend the armscye and hip **H** edges to these marks and draw solid pen lines over the pencil marks, connecting the armscye and hip extensions.

    Measure 3/16 inch inward from these solid lines, making little pencil marks at each measurement. Draw broken pen lines over these marks.

    These measurements create a 3/16-inch seam allowance to each side edge, as well as add the 1-inch all-around "wiggle room." *(Fig.9-5 and Fig.9-6)*

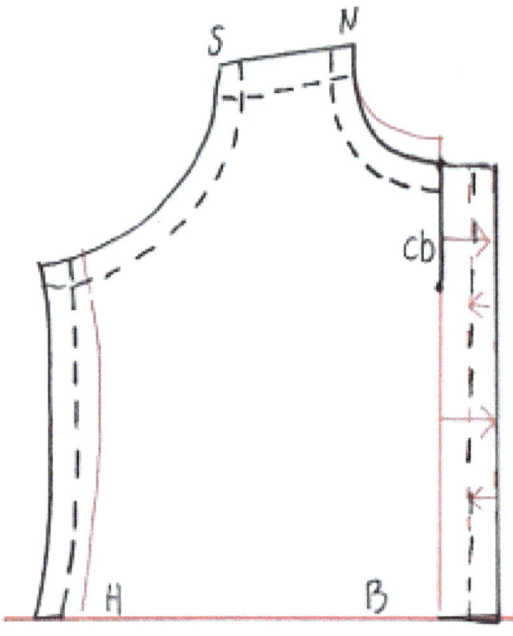

Fig.9-7

11. Draw a 1-inch (3cm) pen line down the back edge of the back shape, starting from the back neck edge. This marks the center back line of a slip-drop-waist bodice pattern. Mark it as **cb**. *(Fig.9-7)*

12. Measure 7/16 inch outward from and along the back edge, making little pencil marks at each measurement. Extend the neck and hip **H** edges to these marks, curving the neck edge extension slightly to match the back neck edge, and draw a solid pen line over the pencil marks, connecting the neck and waist edge extensions.

    Measure 3/16 inch inward along this solid line, making little pencil marks at each measurement. Draw a broken pen line over these marks.

    These measurements create a 3/16-inch back edge seam allowance and a 1/4-inch (6mm) overlap at the center back. *(Fig.9-7)*

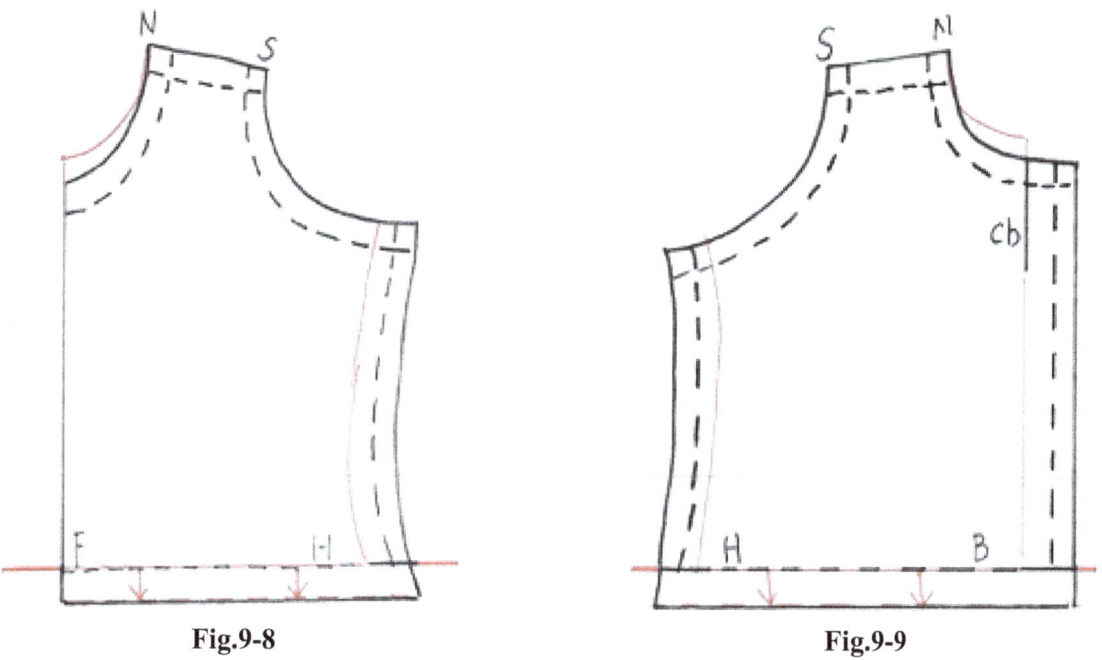

Fig.9-8   Fig.9-9

13. Measure 1/4 inch downward from and along the hip edge **H** of both the front and back shapes (along that first line you drew on the paper), making little pencil marks at each measurement. Extend the slip front, sides, and back edges to these marks and draw solid pen lines over the pencil marks, connecting the front, side, and back edge extensions. Draw broken pen lines over the original pencil tracings (along that first line). You are adding a 1/4-inch waist seam allowance to each edge. *(Fig.9-8 and Fig.9-9)*

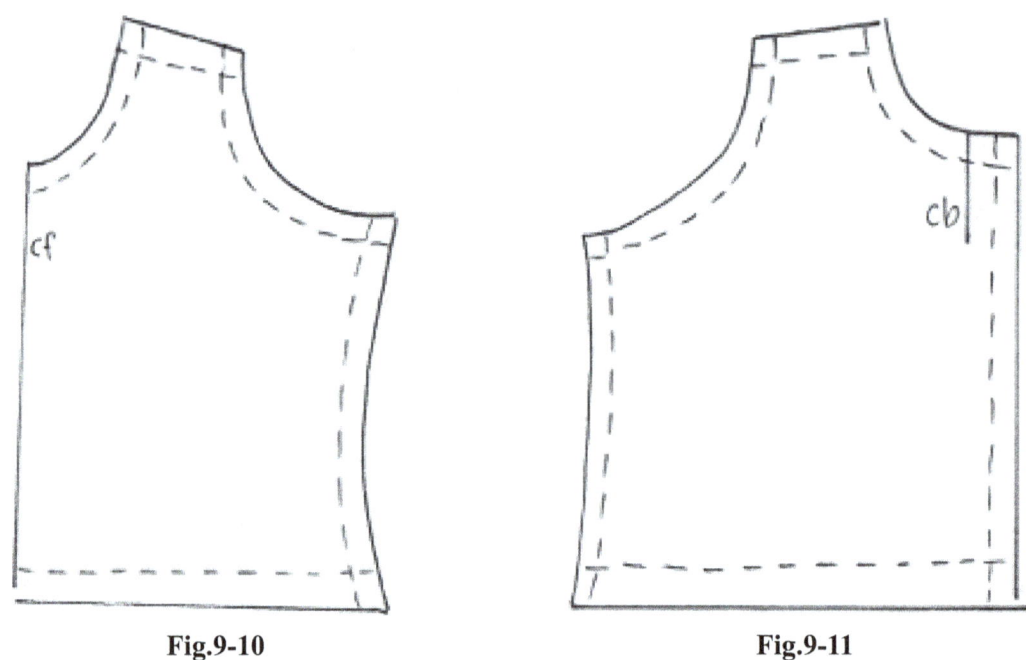

Fig.9-10　　　　　　　　**Fig.9-11**

These drawings *(Fig.9-10 and Fig.9-11)* represent your doll's Front and Back Slip Drop-Waist Bodice Basic Patterns.

Cut out the Front and Back Slip Drop-Waist Bodice Basic Patterns you made for your doll and enjoy sewing a set.

Now, what if your slip drop-waist bodice basic patterns need darts for a better fit against your doll's torso? Here's how to solve that problem.

SLIP DROP-WAIST BODICE WITH DART BASIC PATTERN
Refer to *Fig.10-1* through *Fig.10-11* as examples for drafting your doll's front and back slip drop-waist bodice with dart basic patterns using your bodice with dart basic shapes.
Instructions for a Natural **C** or Empire **E** front and back slip bodice with dart basic patterns are the same, except you start with either **C** or **E** on the drawn line. You will need some clean paper, a ruler, a pencil, and a pen. Remember, for your reference only, the little arrows indicate direction and **red** ink represents pencil lines/marks/arrows.

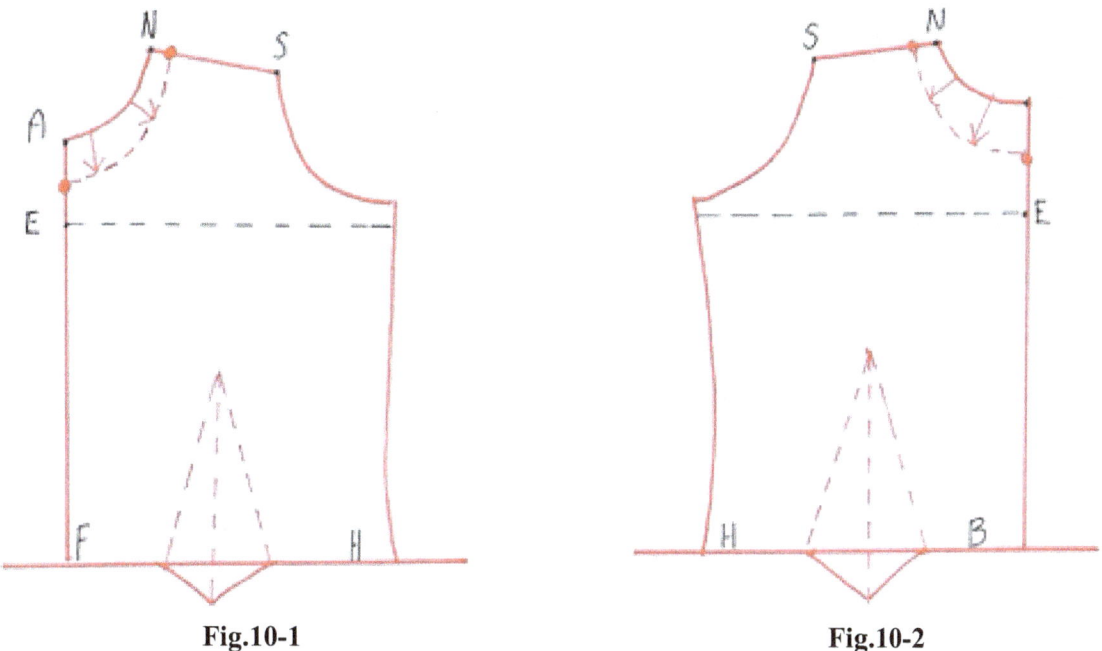

Fig.10-1   **Fig.10-2**

1. Draw a pencil line 2 inches (5cm) up from and across the bottom edge of a clean piece of paper.

2. Set the hip edges **H** of one set of the front and back slip drop-waist bodices with basic dart shapes on the line about 3 inches (8cm) apart and facing away from each other. The bottom of the darts will extend beyond the line. Trace a solid pencil line around each basic shapes. Set the shapes aside. *(Fig.10-1 and Fig.10-2)*

   Because the necklines of the front and back necklines of a slip are not usually very high up around the neck, adjustments to the neck edges of the front and back shapes are needed. Find the measurement **A-E** on your doll's strip. You will be using half of this measurement for the adjustments.

3. Transfer this measurement, half of **A-E**, to the front shape sand back shapes, starting from **A** in the front and the center back neck edge in the back, making a large pencil dot at the end of these measurements. *(Fig.10-1 and Fig.10-2)*

4. Because the neck edge **N** of the shoulder **N-S** is also too close around the neck, adjustments to the shoulder edges of both the front and back shapes are needed here. From **N**, measure 3/16 inch (5mm) inward along each shoulder edge and make a large pencil dot.

5. Draw a broken pencil line from the pencil dots on the shoulder edges down to the large pencil dots on the front and back edges, following the curves of the original pencil tracings as much as possible. These are the basic shapes' new neck edges. *(Fig.10-1 and Fig.10-2)*

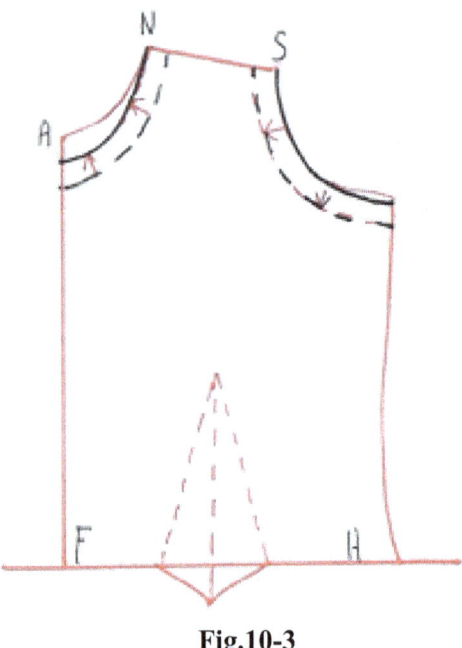
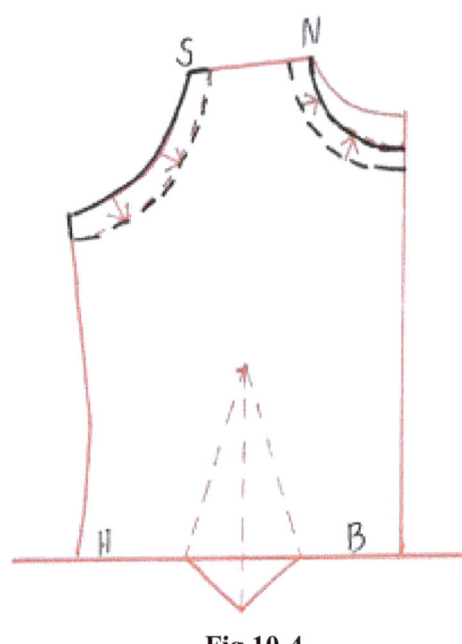

Fig.10-3   **Fig.10-4**

6. Measure 3/16 inch upward from and along each of the new neck edges, making little pencil marks at each measurement. Draw solid pen lines over these marks and broken pen lines over the broken pencil lines of the new necklines. You are adding 3/16-inch seam allowances to each neck edge. *(Fig.10-3 and Fig.10-4)*

7. Measure 3/16 inch inward from and along the traced armscye edge of both the front and back shapes, making little pencil marks at each measurement. Draw broken pen lines over these marks and solid pen lines over the original pencil tracing. You are making 3/16-inch seam allowances inside each armscye edge. *(Fig.10-3 and Fig.10-4)*

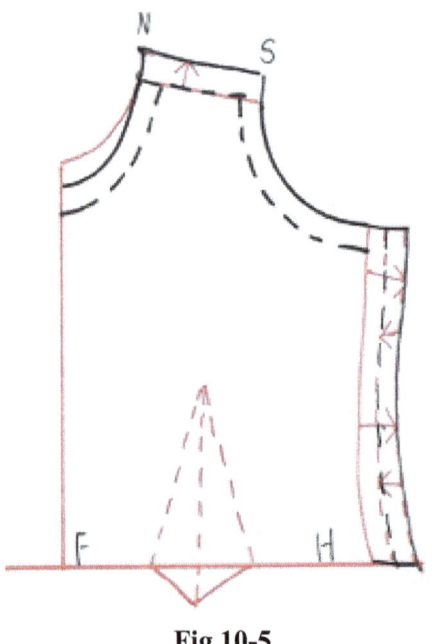
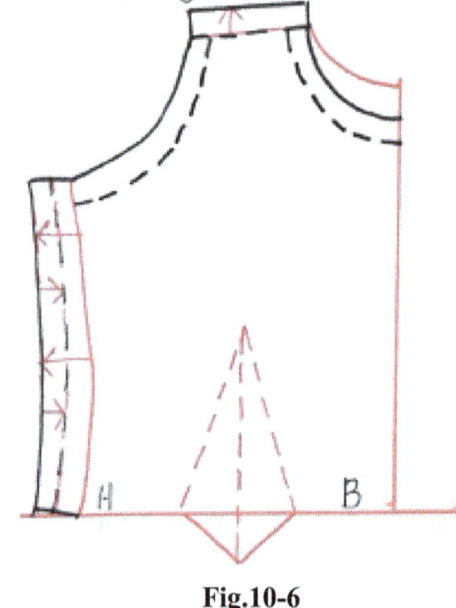

Fig.10-5   **Fig.10-6**

8. Measure 3/16 inch upward from and along the shoulder edges of both the front and back shapes, making little pencil marks at each measurement. Draw solid pen lines over these marks and broken pen lines over the original pencil tracings. You are adding a 3/16-inch seam allowance to each shoulder edge. *(Fig.10-5 and Fig.10-6)*

Just as you add seam allowances to the side edges of the slip bodice front and back shapes without a dart, you should do the same for the slip bodice front and back shapes with darts. A little more width ("wiggle room" all around the torso) is needed; otherwise, the slip drop-waist bodice basic pattern with a dart developed from these shapes will be too tight. After years of sewing for dolls, I decided that a 1-inch (3cm) addition all around was just enough.

9. Measure 7/16 inch (1cm) outward from and along the side edges of both the front and back shapes, making little pencil marks at each measurement. Extend the armscye and hip **H** edges to these marks and draw solid pen lines over the pencil marks, connecting the armscye and hip extensions.

   Measure 3/16 inch inward from these solid lines, making little pencil marks at each measurement. Draw broken pen lines over these marks.

   These measurements create a 3/16-inch seam allowance to each side edge of both the front and back shapes, as well as add the 1-inch all-around "wiggle room." *(Fig.10-5 and Fig.10-6)*

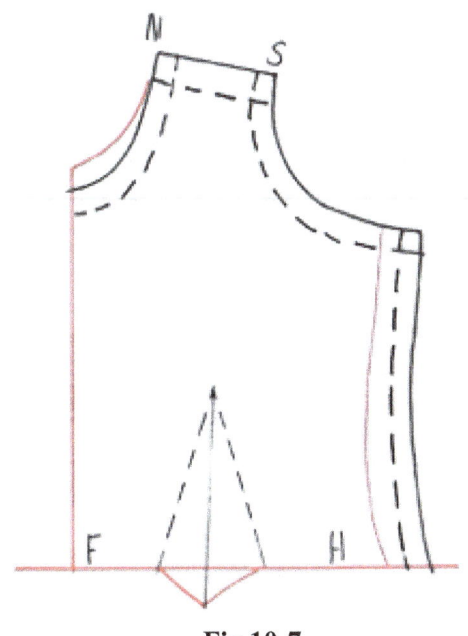

Fig.10-7

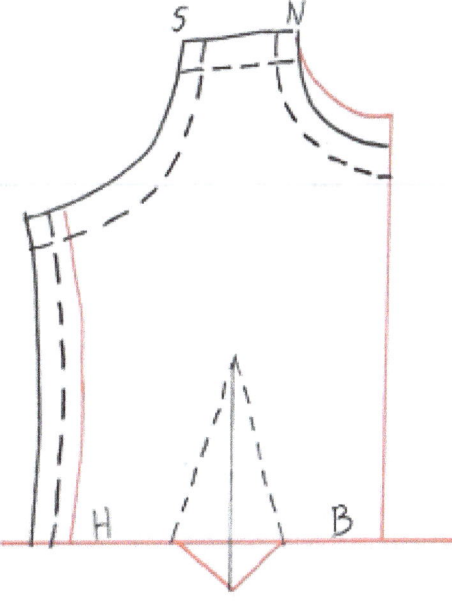

Fig.10-8

10. Draw a broken pen line over the broken pencil side-lines of the darts. These lines, when matched, create the stitching line of the darts. Draw a solid pen line over the middle broken pencil lines. These are the fold-lines of the darts. *(Fig.10-7 and Fig.10-8)*

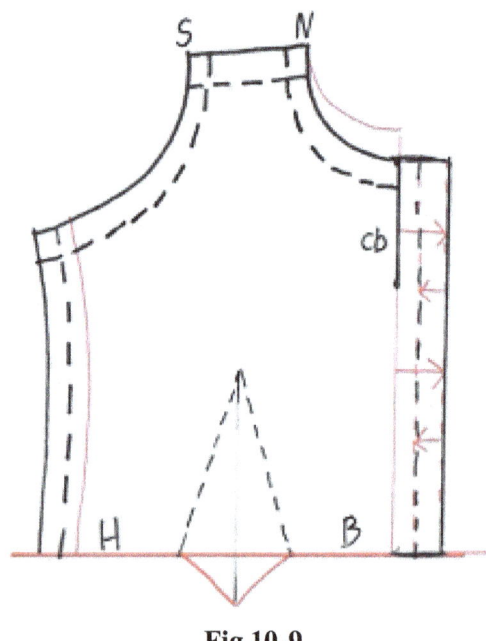

Fig.10-9

11. Draw a 1-inch (3cm) pen line down the back edge of the back shape starting from the back neck edge. This is the center back of a slip-drop waist bodice with a darts pattern. Mark it as **cb**. *(Fig.10-9)*

12. Measure 7/16 inch outward from and along the back edge, making little pencil marks at each measurement. Extend the neck and hip **H** edges to these marks, curving the neck edge extension up a little to match that of the back neck edge. Draw a solid pen line over the pencil marks, connecting the neck and waist edge extensions.

    Measure 3/16 inch inward from and along this solid line, making little pencil marks at each measurement. Draw a broken pen line over these marks.

    These two measurements create a 3/16-inch back edge seam allowance, as well as a 1/4-inch (6mm) overlap at the center back. *(Fig.10-9)*

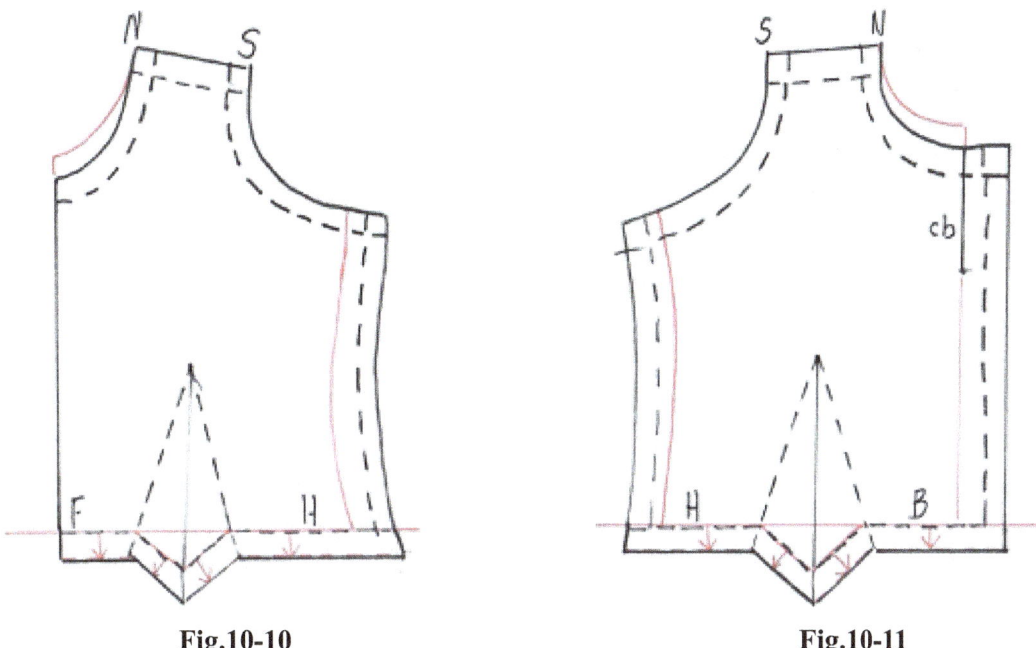

Fig.10-10 **Fig.10-11**

13. Measure 1/4 inch downward from and along each hip edge **H** (including darts) of both the front and back shapes, making little pencil marks at each measurement. Extend the front, sides, and back edges to these marks and draw a solid pen line over the pencil marks, connecting the front, side, and back edge extensions. Draw a broken pen line over the original pencil tracings. Extend the dart lines to the solid line. You have added a 1/4-inch waist seam allowance to the front and back shapes. *(Fig.10-10 and Fig.10-11)*

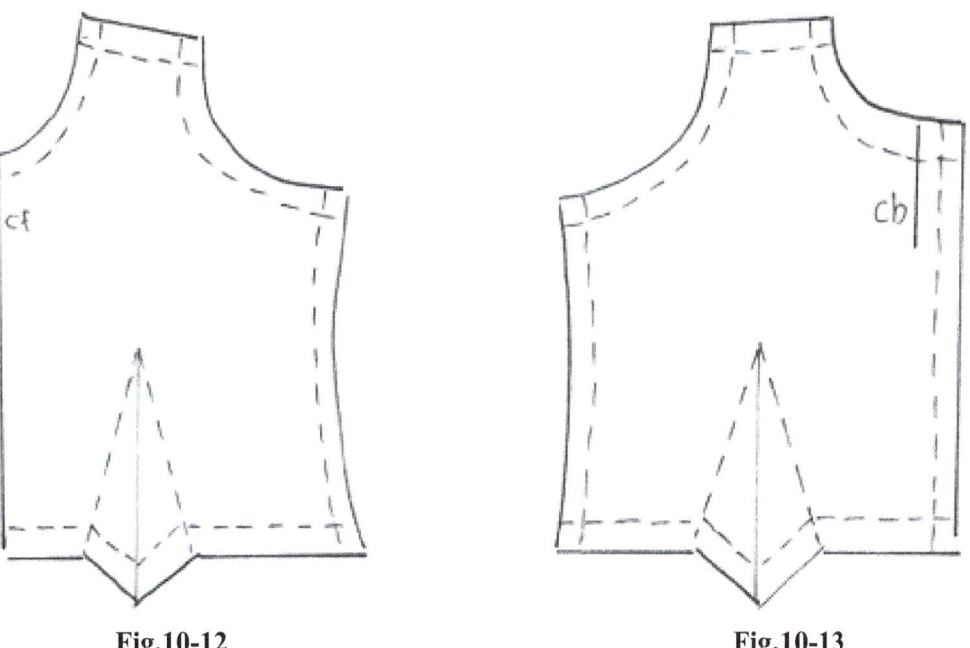

Fig.10-12 **Fig.10-13**

These drawings *(Fig.10-12 and Fig.10-13)* represent your doll's Slip Drop-Waist Bodice with Dart Basic Patterns.

Cut out the Front and Back Slip Drop-Waist Bodice with Darts Basic Patterns you made for your doll and have fun sewing a set.

Dress

Drop-Waist Bodice Basic Pattern

Refer to *Fig.11-1* through *Fig.11-9* as examples for drafting your doll's front and back dress drop-waist bodice basic patterns using your bodice basic shapes.

Instructions for a Natural **C** or Empire **E** front and back dress drop-waist bodice basic patterns are the same, except you start with either **C** or **E** on the drawn line. You will need some clean paper, a ruler, a pencil, and a pen. Remember, for your reference only, the little arrows indicate direction and **red** ink represents pencil lines/marks/arrows.

1. Draw a pencil line 2 inches (5cm) up from and across the bottom edge of a clean piece of paper.

2. Set the hip edges **H** of another set of front and back bodice basic shapes on the line about 3-inches (8cm) apart and facing away from each other. Trace a solid pencil line around the basic shapes. Set the shapes aside.

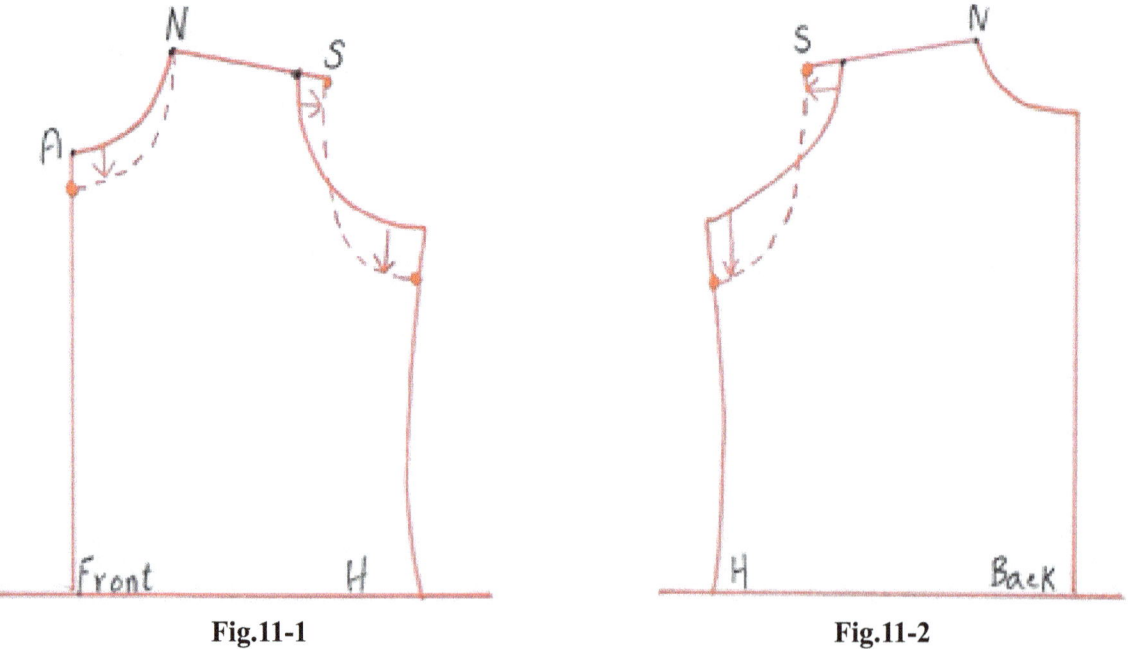

Fig.11-1   Fig.11-2

Because a doll's dress' front neck edge isn't usually right against the neck, an adjustment in the neck edge of the traced front shape is needed. If you want your doll's dress' front neck edge to be bang up against your doll's front neck, skip the next step and proceed with the following step.

3. Decide how much lower you want your doll's front neck edge to be. Starting at **A**, measure downward along the front edge of the shape. Make a large pencil dot at the end of your measurement. Draw a broken curved pencil line from **N** to the large pencil dot. This is the new neck edge of the dress' front shape. *(Fig.11-1)*

The armscye of a dress bodice at the underarm is a bit deeper than that of a slip bodice. Also, the shoulder at **S** of a dress bodice covers more of the top of a doll's arm than that of a slip bodice. An adjustment to the basic dress shape is needed at these two places.

4. Decide the depth you want for your dress bodice at the underarm. Beginning at the armscye edge, measure this depth downward along the side edges of both the front and back shapes, making a large pencil dot at the end of the measurement. *(Fig.11-1 and Fig.11-2)*

5. Measure the top of your doll's shoulder from the neck at **N** to the top of your doll's arm. Transfer this measurement to the **N-S** edge of both the front and back shapes, extending **S** to the end of your measurements, making a large pencil dot at the ends. *(Fig.11-1 and Fig.11-2)*

6. Draw broken curved pencil lines downward from the large pencil dots at the new **S** to the large pencil dots on the side edges. These are the new armscye edges of the front and back dress basic bodice shapes. *(Fig.11-1 and Fig.11-2)*

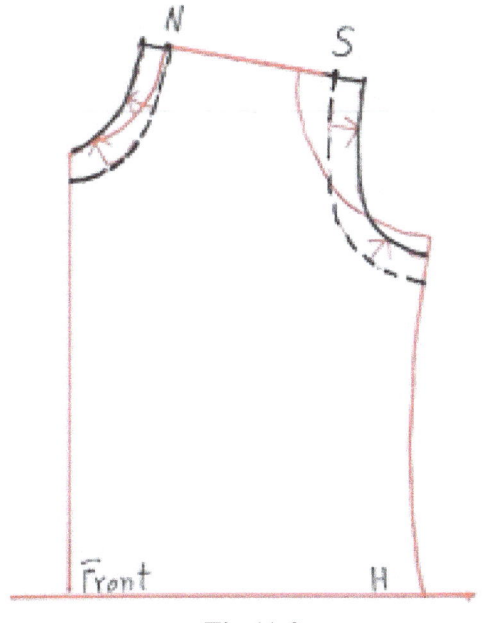

Fig.11-3

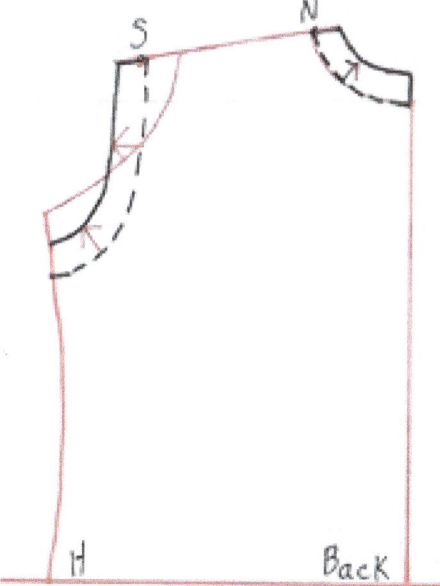

Fig.11-4

7. Measure 3/16 inch (5mm) outward from and along the front shape's new neck edge and the back shape's traced neck edge, making little pencil marks at each measurement. Draw solid pen lines over these marks and broken pen lines over the penciled front neck edge and the traced back neck edge. You are adding a 3/16-inch seam allowance to each neck edge. *(Fig.11-3 and Fig.11-4)*

8. Measure 3/16 inch outward from and along the new front and back shape armscye edges, making little pencil marks at each measurement. Draw solid pen lines over these marks and broken pen lines over the new armscye broken pencil lines. You are adding a 3/16-inch seam allowance to each armscye. *(Fig.11-3 and Fig.11-4)*

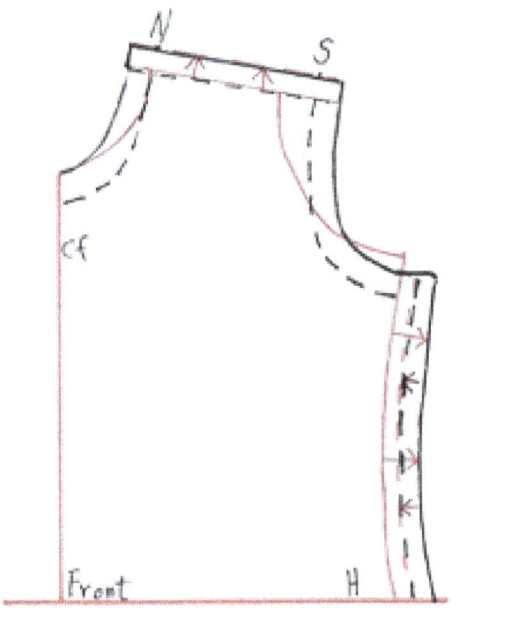

Fig.11-5   **Fig.11-6**

9. Measure 3/16 inch upward from and along the front and back shape shoulder edges, making little pencil marks at each measurement. Draw a solid pen line over these marks and a broken pen line over the pencil-traced marks. You are adding a 3/16-inch seam allowance to each shoulder edge. *(Fig.11-5 and Fig.11-6)*

Along with adding seam allowances to the side edges of the dress bodice front and back basic shapes, a little more width ("wiggle room" all around the torso) is needed, or the dress drop-waist bodice basic pattern developed from these shapes will be too tight a fit over a slip bodice. After years of sewing for dolls, I decided that a 1–1/4-inch (3cm) addition was just enough. If you wish for more or less, use your measurement instead.

10. Measure 1/2 inch (1cm) outward from and along the side edges of both the front and back shapes, making little pencil marks at each measurement. Extend the armscye and hip **H** edges

to these marks and draw a solid pen line over the pencil marks, connecting the armscye and hip edge extensions.

Measure 3/16 inch inward from and along these solid lines, making little pencil marks at each measurement. Draw a broken pen line over these marks.

These two measurements create a 3/16-inch (5mm) seam allowance to the side edges of both the front and back shapes, as well as add the 1–1/4-inch all-around "wiggle room." *(Fig.11-5 and Fig.11-6)*

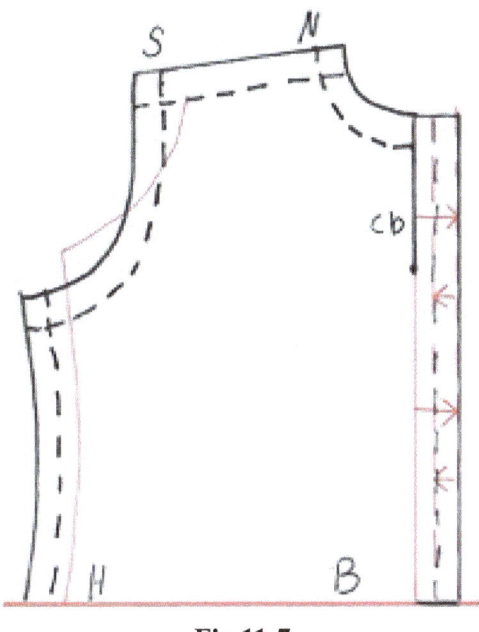

Fig.11-7

11. With the pen, draw a 1-inch (3cm) line downward along the back edge of the back shape starting from the back neck edge. This is the center back of a dress basic drop-waist bodice pattern. Mark it as **cb**. *(Fig.11-7)*

12. Measure 7/16 inch (1cm) outward from and along the back edge of the back shape, making little pencil marks at each measurement. Extend the back neck and hip **H** edges to these marks, curving the neck edge extension slightly to "mirror" the back shape neck edge. Draw a solid pen line through the pencil marks, connecting the back neck and hip extensions.

Measure 3/16 inch (5mm) inward from and along this solid line, making little pencil marks at each measurement. Draw a broken pen line over these marks.

These two measurements create a 3/16-inch back seam allowance, as well as allow for a 1/4-inch overlap at the center back. *(Fig.11-7)*

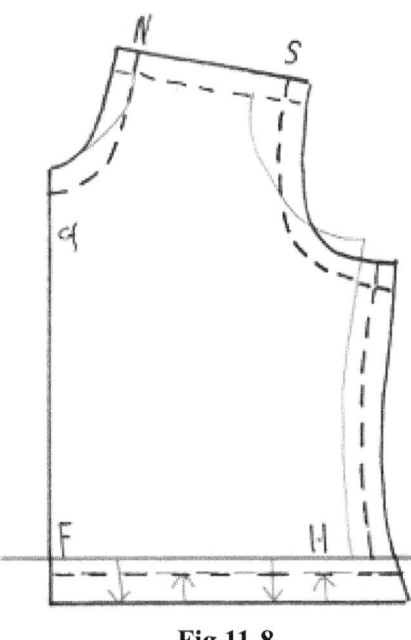
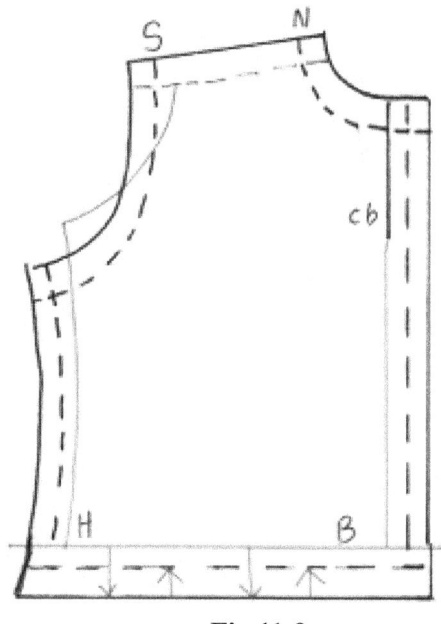

Fig.11-8   **Fig.11-9**

13. Measure 7/16 inch (1.1cm) downward from and along the hip edge **H** of the front and back shapes, making little pencil marks at each measurement. Extend the front, sides, and back edges down to these pencil marks and draw a solid line over them, connecting the front, side, and back edge extensions.

Measure 1/4 inch upward from and along this solid line, making little pencil marks at each measurement. Draw a broken pen line over these marks.

These two measurements create a 1/4-inch waist seam allowance to both shapes, as well as an extra 3/16-inch length to a drop-waist dress bodice to fit nicely over an undergarment. *(Fig.11-8 and Fig.11-9)*

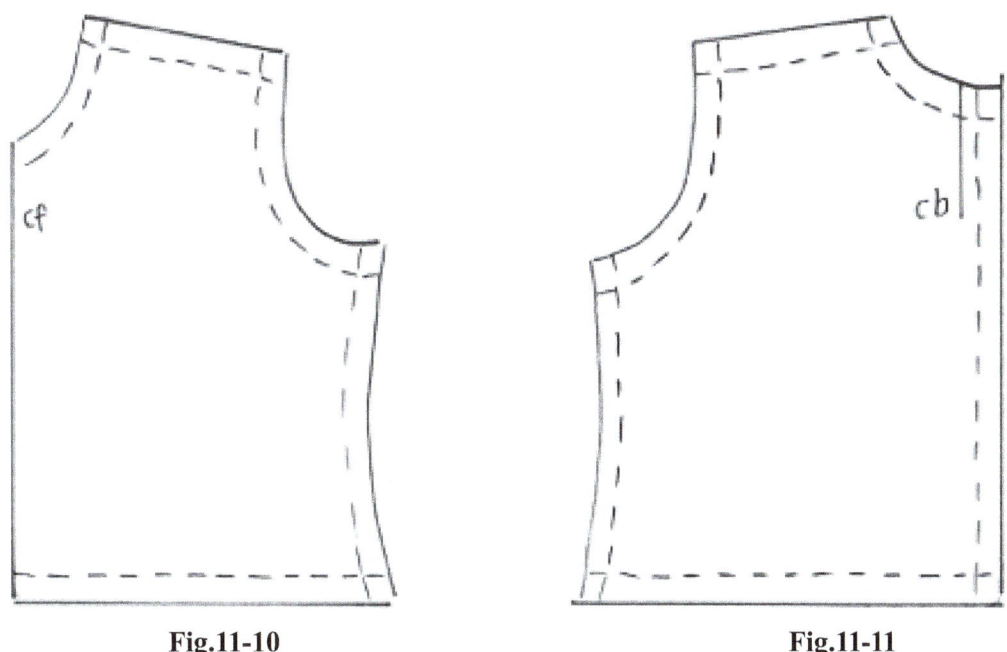

Fig.11-10 **Fig.11-11**

These drawings represent your doll's Front and Back Dress Drop-Waist Bodice Basic Patterns. Cut them out and have fun sewing a set.

As with the slip pattern, what if your doll's dress drop-waist bodice basic pattern needs darts to fit better against your doll's torso? Here's how to solve that problem.

DROP-WAIST BODICE WITH DART BASIC PATTERN
Refer to *Fig.12-1* through *Fig.12-16* for examples of drafting front and back dress drop-waist bodice with dart basic patterns using your bodice with dart basic shapes.

Instructions for a Natural **C** or Empire **E** front and back dress drop waist bodice with dart basic patterns are the same, except you start with either **C** or **E** on the drawn line. You will need some clean paper, a ruler, a pencil, and a pen. Remember, for your reference only, the little arrows indicate direction and red ink represents pencil lines/marks/arrows.

1. Draw a pencil line 2 inches (5cm) up from and across the bottom edge of a clean piece of paper.

2. Set the hip edges **H** of another set of front and back bodices with dart basic shapes on the line, about 3 inches (8cm) apart and facing away from each other. The edge of the darts in each shape will be slightly below the drawn line. Trace a solid pencil line around the bodice shapes and set the shapes aside. *(Fig.12-1 and Fig.12-2)*

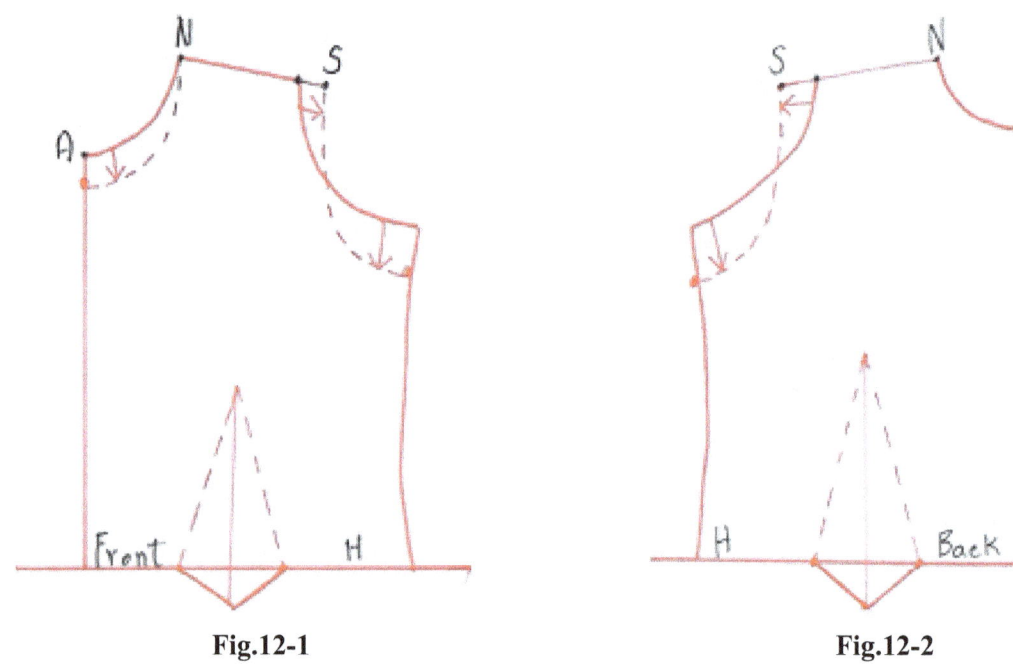

Fig.12-1   **Fig.12-2**

Because a doll's dress' front neck edge isn't usually right against the neck, an adjustment in the neck edge of the traced front shape is needed. If you want your doll's dress' front neck edge to be bang up against your doll's front neck, then skip the next step and proceed with the following step.

3. Decide how much lower you want your doll's neck edge to be. Starting at **A**, measure downward along the front edge of the shape, and make a large pencil dot at the end of your measurement. Draw a broken curved line from **N** to the large dot. This is the new neck edge of the dress' front shape. *(Fig.12-1)*

4. Decide the depth you want for your dress bodice at the underarm. Measure this depth downward along the side edges of both the front and back shapes beginning at the armscye edge, making a large pencil dot at the end of the measurement. *(Fig.12-1 and Fig.12-2)*

5. Measure the top of your doll's shoulder from the neck at **N** to the top of your doll's arm. Transfer this measurement to the **N-S** edge of both the front and back shapes, extending **S** to the end of your measurements and making a large pencil dot at the ends. *(Fig.12-1 and Fig.12-2)*

6. With the pencil, draw broken curved lines downward from the large pencil dots at the new **S** to the large pencil dots on the side edges. These are the new front and back dress bodice shape armscye edges. *(Fig.12-1 and Fig.12-2)*

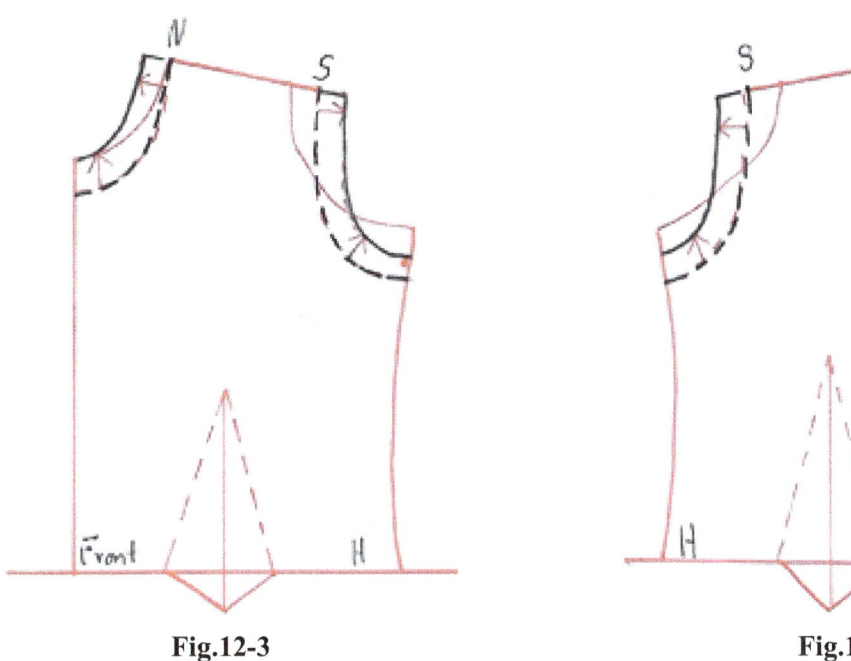

| Fig.12-3 | Fig.12-4 |

7. Measure 3/16 inch outward from and along the front shape new neck edge and the back shape traced neck edge, making little pencil marks at each measurement. Draw a solid line over these marks and a broken pen line over the penciled front neck edge and the traced back neck edge. You are adding a 3/16-inch seam allowance to each neck edge. *(Fig.12-3 and Fig.12-4)*

8. Measure 3/16 inch outward from and along the new armscye edges of both the front and back bodices, making little pencil marks at each measurement. Draw solid pen lines over these marks and broken pen lines over the broken pencil lines. You are adding a 3/16-inch seam allowance to each armscye. *(Fig.12-3 and Fig.12-4)*

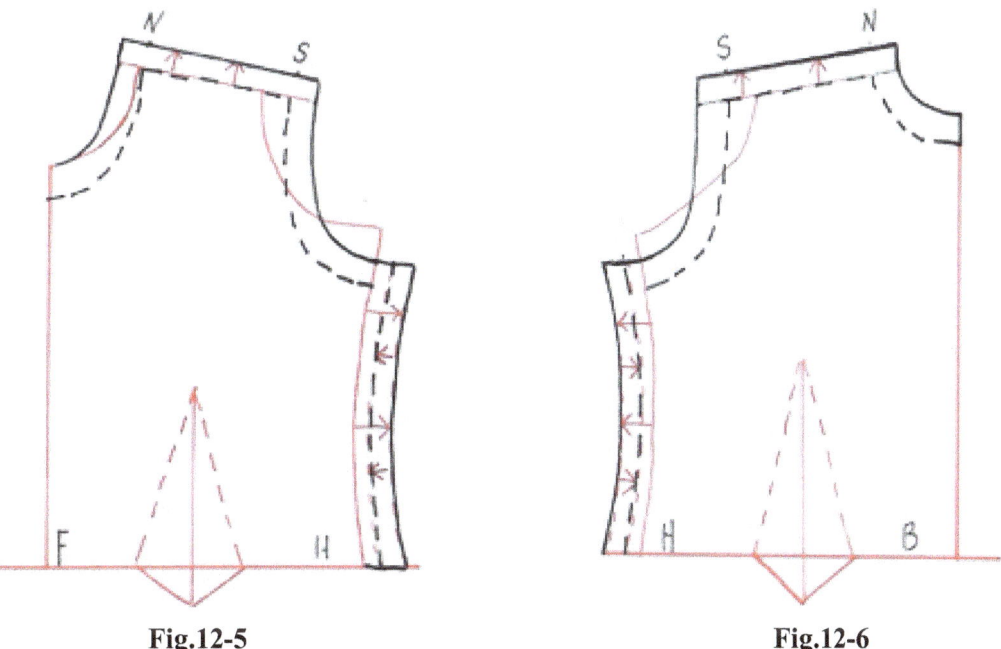

| Fig.12-5 | Fig.12-6 |

9. Measure 3/16 inch upward from and along the shoulder edges of the front and back shapes, making little pencil marks at each measurement. Draw a solid pen line over these marks and a broken pen line over the pencil-traced marks. You are adding a 3/16-inch seam allowance to each shoulder edge. *(Fig.12-5 and Fig.12-6)*

   Just as you add seam allowances to the side edges of the dress bodice front and back basic shapes without a dart, you should do the same for the slip bodice front and back shapes with darts. A little more width ("wiggle room" all around the torso) is needed, or the dress drop-waist bodice basic pattern developed from these shapes will be too tight over a slip bodice. After years of sewing for dolls, I decided that a 1–1/4-inch (3cm) addition was just enough. If you wish for more or less, use those measurements instead.

10. Measure 1/2 inch (1cm) outward from and along both the front and back shape side edges, making little pencil marks at each measurement. Extend the armscye and hip **H** edges to these marks and draw a solid pen line over the pencil marks, connecting the armscye and hip edge extensions.

    Measure 3/16 inch inward from and along these solid lines, making little pencil marks at each measurement. Draw a broken pen line over these marks.

    These two measurements create a 3/16-inch seam allowance to the side edges of both the front and back shapes, as well as add the 1–1/4-inch all-around "wiggle room." *(Fig.12-5 and Fig.12-6)*

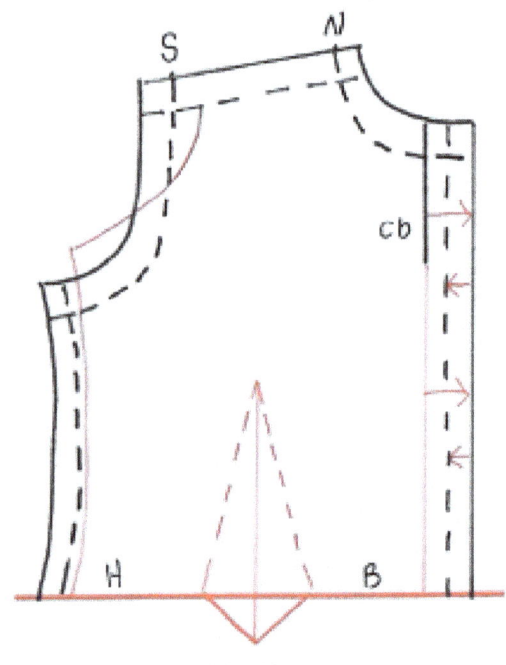

Fig.12-7

11. With the pen, draw a 1-inch (3cm) line downward along the back edge of the back shape starting from the back neck edge. This is the center back of a dress basic drop-waist bodice pattern. Mark it as **cb**. *(Fig.12-7)*

12. Measure 7/16 inch (1cm) outward from and along the back edge of the back shape, making little pencil marks at each measurement. Extend the back neck and hip **H** edges to these marks, curving the neck edge extension up a bit to "mirror" the back shape neck edge. Draw a solid pen line through the pencil marks, connecting the back neck and hip extensions.

    Measure 3/16 inch inward from and along this solid line, making little pencil marks at each measurement. Draw a broken pen line over these marks.

    These measurements create a 3/16-inch back seam allowance, as well as allow for a 1/4-inch overlap at the center back. *(Fig.12-7)*

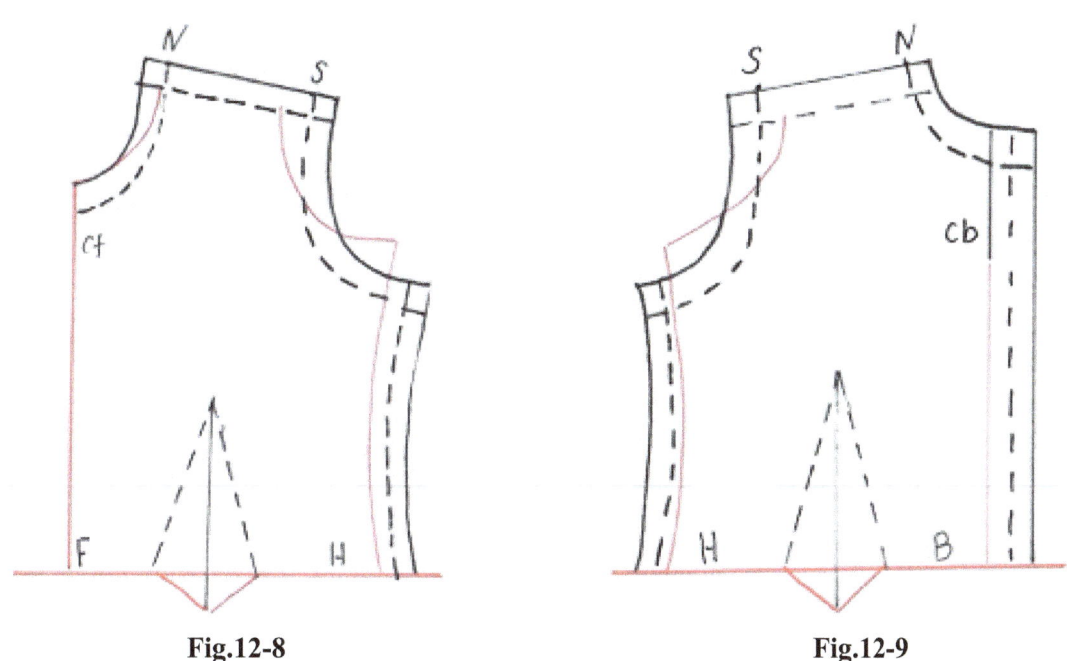

Fig.12-8　　　　　　　　**Fig.12-9**

13. Draw broken pen lines over the broken side-lines of the darts. These lines, when matched, create the stitching line of the darts. Draw solid pen lines over the broken middle lines. These are the fold-lines of the darts. *(Fig.12-8 and Fig.12-9)*

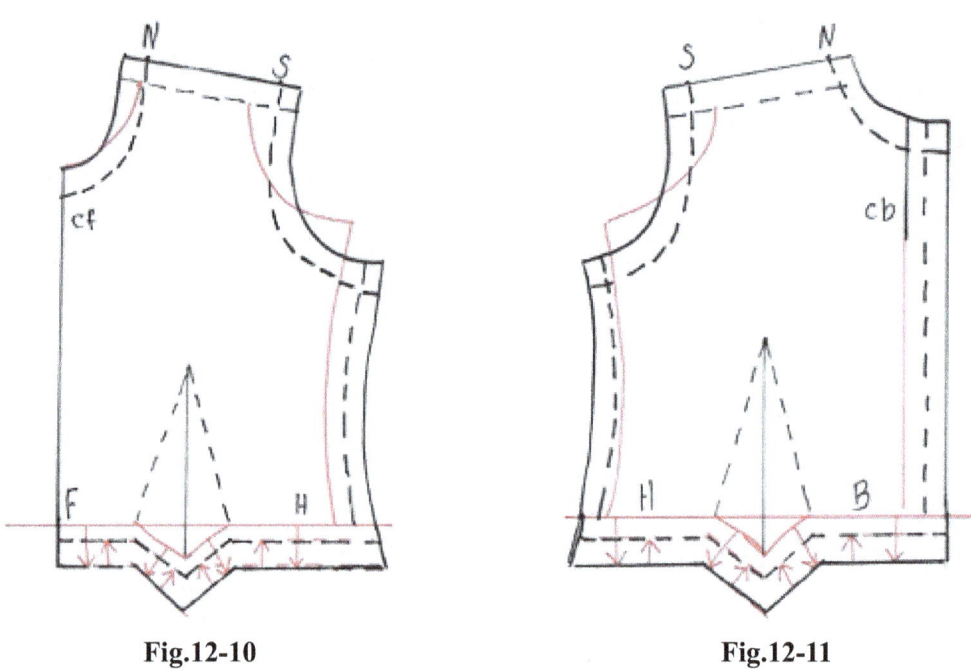

Fig.12-10 **Fig.12-11**

14. Measure 7/16 inch downward from and along the bottom edge **H** (including darts) of the front and back shapes, making little pencil marks at each measurement. Extend the shapes' front, sides, and back edges down to these marks and draw a solid pen line over the pencil marks, connecting the front, side, and back edge extensions.

   Measure 1/4 inch upward from and along the solid lines, making little pencil marks at each measurement. Draw broken pen lines over these marks.

   These two measurements create a 1/4-inch waist seam allowance to both the front and back shapes, as well as an extra 3/16-inch length to allow a drop-waist dress bodice to fit nicely over an undergarment. *(Fig.12-10 and Fig.12-11)*

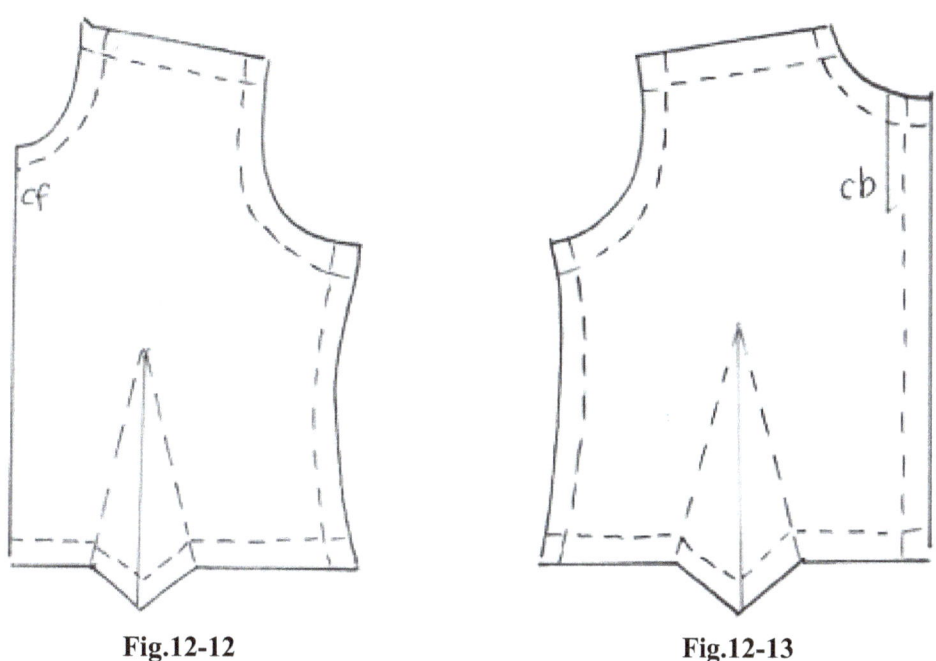

Fig.12-12   **Fig.12-13**

These drawings *(Fig.12-12 and Fig.12-13)* represent your doll's Front and Back Dress Drop Waist Bodice with Dart Basic Patterns.

Cut out the Front and Back Dress Drop-Waist Bodice with Darts Basic Patterns you made for your doll and have fun sewing a set.

SLEEVE BASIC PATTERN

Refer to *Fig.13-1* and *Fig.13-2* for examples of drafting a sleeve basic pattern using your basic sleeve shape. Remember, for your reference only, the little arrows indicate direction and **red** ink represents pencil lines/marks/arrows.

The basic sleeve shape, as it is, even with added underarm seam allowances, will be too tight around the doll's arm. Not a good fit. You probably wouldn't be able to fit such a sleeve over a doll's hands. So, we add some width to this shape. The added width depends on how full you want your doll's sleeve to be. From this plain sleeve basic shape, you will be developing a plain sleeve basic pattern, from which you can develop any other type of sleeve you desire.

1. Once again, draw a horizontal pencil line across the bottom of a clean piece of paper. Place the wrist edge of one of your basic sleeve shapes on the drawn line and make a large pencil dot at **S** on the paper, labeling it **S**. Remove the basic sleeve shape. Draw a vertical pencil line downward from **S** to the drawn pencil line on the paper. Mark the end of this line with a large pencil dot, labeling it **W**. *(Fig.13-1)*

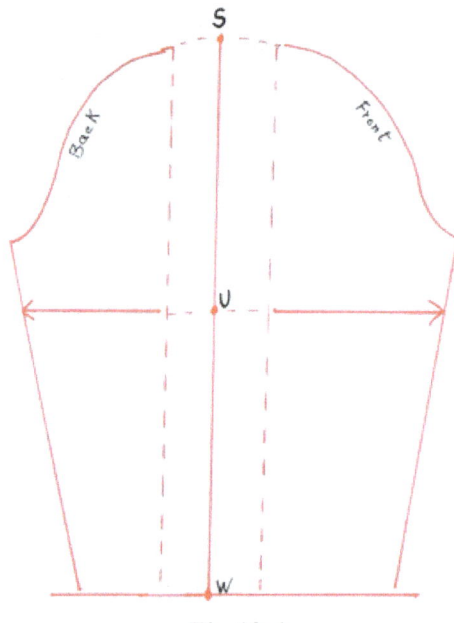

Fig.13-1

2. Using the measurement of **S-U** found on your doll's strip, measure this distance on the **S-W** line, starting at **S.** At the end of the **S-U** measurement, make a large pencil dot, label it **U.** *(Fig.13-1)*

3. Fold your basic shape over from **S** down, matching the wrist edges **W**, and crease the fold. Cut the shape along the fold. You will notice that the back part of the sleeve is slightly narrower than the front part. This is OK. Remember, **S** is not centered at the top of a sleeve cap; it is the point where the sleeve cap matches the shoulder seam of a bodice armscye.

4. Place the **W** edge of the two parts on the drawn pencil line. Space them apart just enough so that your desired width measures from the front underarm edge to the back underarm edge at the **U** level (arrows), not within the space between the two parts. Each part should also be positioned the same distance from the drawn **S-W** line. When in place, make a solid pencil tracing of the two parts, connecting them at the top. *(Fig.13-1)*

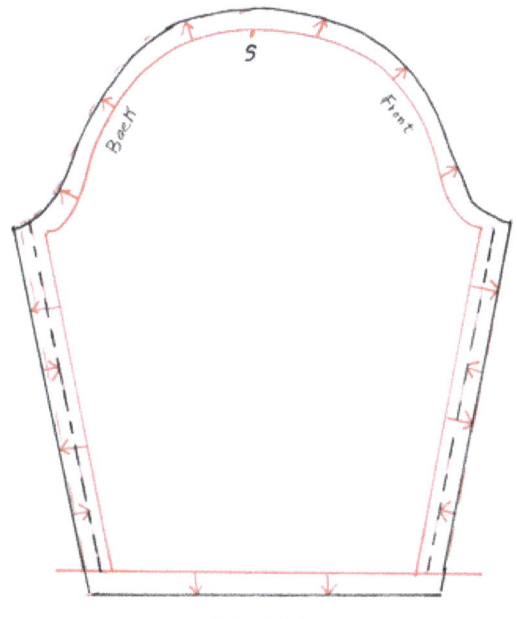

Fig.13-2

5. Measure 3/16 inch (5mm) upward from and along the top (cap) edge of the shape, making little pencil marks at each measurement. Draw a solid pen line through these marks and a broken pen line over the pencil tracing. You are adding a 3/16-inch seam allowance to the cap of the shape. *(Fig.13-2)*

6. Measure 3/8 inch (1cm) outward from and along each underarm edge, making little pencil marks at each measurement. Extend the armscye and wrist edge to these marks and draw a solid pen line over the pencil marks, connecting the armscye and wrist lines.

   Measure 3/16 inch inward from and along these solid lines, making little pencil marks at each measurement. Draw a broken pen line through these marks.

   These two measurements create a 3/16-inch seam allowance for each underarm edge, as well as enough width to match the added width to the dress bodice side edges. *(Fig.13-2)*

7. Measure 3/16 inch downward from and along the **W** line between the outer underarm edges, making little pencil marks at each measurement. Draw a solid pen line over these marks and a broken pen line over the **W** line. You have added a 3/16-inch seam allowance at the wrist edge. *(Fig.13-2)*

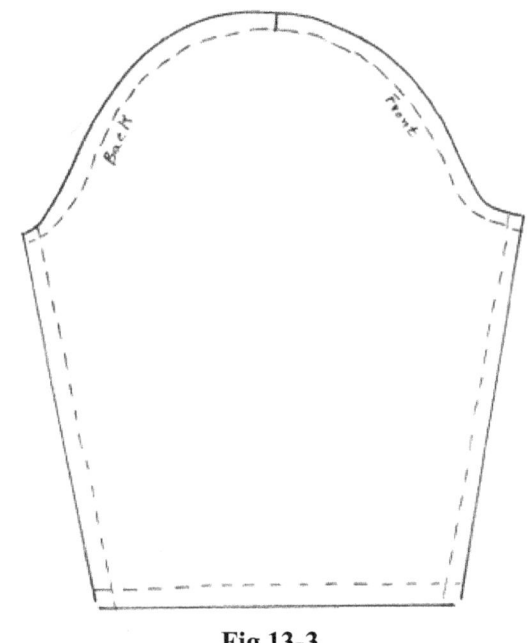

Fig.13-3

This drawing represents your doll's Basic Sleeve Pattern.

Cut out the Basic Sleeve Pattern you made for your doll and have fun making a dress with sleeves that fit the Dress's Basic Drop-Waist Pattern, either with or without the Dart.

You are now ready to create a facing, or a hem, or add lace edging to this plain sleeve pattern. If you wish for a fuller sleeve ending with a drawstring or cuff, follow the instructions for adding a drawstring or cuff in some of the following **Q** and **A**s.

Now that you have your basic patterns, let's get down to sewing. The rest of this book is dedicated to Sewing for Dolls. If you are looking for a specific question, the Table of Contents will help you find it.

Happy Sewing!

Semple Answers to Questions on Sewing for Dolls

A Few Notes:
After sewing for several years as a couturiere dressmaker, reducing my skills to "doll-size" was quite a challenge. I had to learn to think small: patterns, fabrics, stitching lengths, machine needles, seams, everything—even scissors!

Starting with patterns, I figured out that it was easier to hold a small pattern piece pinned to a piece of fabric just big enough for the pattern, and then cut the pattern out with a small pair of scissors. This was much easier than laying the pattern down on the fabric and trying to cut around it, which often resulted in screwing up the fabric while cutting. Been there? It was so easy to cut around curves and sharp corners. Was I wasting fabric? Well, yes, but only a small amount. Saving my sanity was more important. To avoid the drastic mistake of cutting two pieces instead of one on a fold, I drew a red ink line on all cut-on-fold lines so I wouldn't forget. And I never use the fold in the fabric as it comes off a bolt. That fold is almost permanent, often faded, and will not always iron out, especially in the vintage fabrics I use for mine and my clients' dolls.

Fabrics are another consideration. Here, again, you must think small in terms of prints, stripes, and plaids. Also, the weight of fabrics is important. Look for lightweight vintage fabrics: cotton prints, silks, satins, velvets, velveteens, sateens, some corduroys, wools, batistes, lawns, even nainsook, which is very rare, but, oh, so dainty. Try to find fabrics that are similar to the era your dolls represent.

As for the length of the stitch, it will take a little practice and experimenting with your sewing machine. Setting the sewing machine stitch length to twelve (12) stitches per inch works very well with most dolls' clothing. Setting the sewing machine to fourteen (14) to sixteen (16) stitches per inch for small dolls is best. Of course, with antique reproduction dolls' clothing, most of the machine stitches would not be visible, but sometimes they are and should be a "natural" length in relation to the size of the doll. Think of how big you are in relation to the doll and how the average length of visible stitches looks on your own clothing when comparing them to those of dolls' clothing. What's OK on your clothing would be huge on a doll's!

For most dolls' sewing, the small machine size #9 needle is best, though occasionally, if making something out of a heavier fabric such as wool or velveteen, use a size #11. And change the needle often. Because #9 is small, it will develop "burrs" more easily and will pick at threads, pulling them and making little puckers in the fabric. They also become very dull and won't go into the fabric easily. My recommendation is to replace the needle every time you start a new project, sometimes even changing it during a project.

Most seams in dolls' garments should be kept from 1/8 inch (3mm) to 3/16 inch (5mm) or 1/4 inch (6mm), depending on the size of the dolls and the garments you are sewing. When making French seams, keep within the total 3/16-inch seam allowance. A fine dressmaker can make very small 1/8-inch French seams by hand, as stitching these tiny French seams by machine renders them a little stiff. These look very nice and are dainty on the fine lawn, nainsook, or batiste underwear, especially on very small dolls. The 1/4-inch seams are mostly for those containing a gathered edge, as in a slip or dress waist seam.

"Crawly" fabrics (silk velvets and chiffons) can be controlled with a little temporary spray adhesive and some tear-away paper or tissue paper. Even a light shot of hairspray will work. Soft tissue or paper towel sheets won't do as they are too soft and tear too easily. Bear in mind, though, that the use of any paper will dull the machine needle faster, so you might have to change the needle more often when sewing with "crawly" fabrics. Spray the paper with the temporary adhesive and place the fabric piece on the paper. If you are sewing a seam, first baste the two edges together, then place the garment piece on the treated paper. I strongly recommend that you baste, baste, and BASTE while sewing these small garments. It helps to keep small pieces together when working with them. And do use a thimble.

Scissors? Yes. You need small and medium-sized scissors, as well as a way to keep them sharp and snag-free. Cutting out small pattern pieces is work and hard on the hands if you have a lot of it. Large scissors just won't do. Remember, you are working with small stuff here: small curves, small corners, short straight edges. You need small tools to work with. Large tools used for human sewing are just too unwieldy.

Sewing Center Supplies
A suggested list of supplies you should have on hand at your sewing center:

- A lamp to shine over your sewing table. Sometimes, daylight or sunlight is much too bright and does not shine where you want it to.
- A magnifying glass (on a gooseneck or attached to an adjustable position work light) to use when sewing very fine stitches, pulling out fine stitches, or even threading needles!

- A peel 'n stick measuring tape to stick to the front edge of your sewing table, so you won't always be reaching for that often-missing cloth or soft plastic measuring tape. It's very handy when measuring a small skirt length, a piece of trim, or a piece of lace.
- A pair of bent-nosed (medical) forceps. These are useful for turning small garments and reaching into tight areas to turn or pull through shoulder areas, small armholes, etc.
- Several long pearl-headed pins (old hat pins work great!) are ideal for picking threads and pulling out small corners.
- A small metal ruler with a closely fitted slide is perfect for even measurements of small hems or sewing lines for laces and trims.
- A roll of thin tear-away paper serves as a stabilizer for thin fabrics.
- Temporary spray adhesive holds "crawly" fabrics to the stabilizer when sewing.
- A fabric marker (that fades) is useful for marking the placement of trims, hems, sewing lines, etc.
- A white fabric marker for dark fabrics brushes off easily.
- A box of long thin silk pins as they don't leave noticeable holes in the fabric.
- A magnetic pin holder keeps pins organized and under control.
- A clear plastic 15-inch (38cm) ruler is essential for measuring and making straight lines when creating or altering a pattern. Sometimes, you need to see through the ruler.
- A sharp #2 soft lead pencil is useful for marking trim or lace placement lines when the fabric marker isn't suitable, or for altering or creating new pattern pieces. Avoid using a pen near your sewing table!
- A roll of clear sticky tape is handy for making or altering patterns.
- Some paper, of course. Printing paper works well.
- A roll of paper towels is useful for draping around a doll for pattern-making.
- A pincushion for your various sized hand sewing needles and long hatpins keeps them clean and free of rust, as they can rust when not used frequently.
- Strawberry emery keeps your needles and silk pins sharp and free of burrs. It is not very effective with machine needles, though.
- A thimble helps push a sewing needle through the fabric, preventing the thread-filled eye of the needle from being pushed into your finger. Ouch!
- A dog comb is ideal for combing mohair when repairing, resetting, or making new wigs. It is gentler on a doll's hair than a regular comb. Never use a brush!
- A small tube or container of some sort of fray check prevents the edges of some fabrics from fraying while sewing.
- A fabric glue stick keeps small trims in place while sewing without needing pins that might otherwise get in the way.
- A small hard cardboard tube wrapped in soft flannel is useful for pressing small sleeve seams.
- A small bottle of hydrogen peroxide and a few cotton swabs help with those all-too-common small blood smears left on a sewing project by a sharp pin prick.
- A "spaghetti" maker for turning bias when making "rat-tail" trims or ties.
- An old flat-bristled toothbrush is useful for brushing lint off napped fabrics or brushing seams of napped fabrics.

- A fine-wired needle threader is helpful when your eyes don't cooperate while trying to thread a needle, especially a fine needle with a tiny eye.
- A container of spray-starch for limp cotton fabrics.
- A piece of white cotton fabric to cover the ironing board when pressing starched sewing prevents the starch from getting into the ironing board cover.
- Small terry cloth towels are useful for wrapping spray-starched items to evenly distribute the starch or for pressing velvet (right-side-down).
- Large old mugs (that have chips or cracks, rendering them useless for drinking) are convenient for storing fabric markers, pencils, metal rulers, dog combs, and any other tall objects that would otherwise clutter your sewing table. You'd be surprised how many items you'll put in them. They are heavy and don't fall over easily.

Items to keep *near the bathroom sink*. (These can become conversation pieces, making guests wonder, "Whaaa …..?")

- A small plastic tub for soaking old fabrics when removing stains or whitening them.
- A stainless steel teaspoon for mixing an enzyme stain remover and water.
- A small strainer to strain the enzyme stain remover and water. The undissolved crystals, when in contact with fabric, can burn holes into it.
- A small plastic cup for mixing the enzyme stain remover and water.
- A small eye dropper for adding small amounts of bleach to water when whitening old fabrics. Ever tried to get a drop of bleach from a one-gallon jug?

Now that you have this list, you're well on your way to finding your own ways to make sewing easier and more fun and growing your own list.

The following collection of questions (**Q**) comes from many doll enthusiasts who asked them via phone, letter, email, at a doll club meeting, a doll show, or through chance person-to-person contact. I've answered (**A**) them all using my experience as a professional couturier for both human and doll clients. Some questions on the same or similar subjects have been combined into a single answer.

Note: If I include a Fig., or two, with my answers, for your reference only, the little arrows show the direction of additions or deletions in patterns, and all pencil marks/lines/arrows in a Fig. are represented by red ink. Paper or fabric included in a Fig. is represented by blue ink. Pen marks/lines/digits in a Fig. are represented by black ink.

A Fig. is a line drawing, created to show you how to do something which is hard to do with a photo. If the line drawings appear not to scale and look a bit strange, bear with me. I drew them to provide as clear an example of my instructions as possible.

On Patterns

DRAWERS

KNEE DRAWSTRING

Q
I have a commercial pattern for a pair of drawers that fit my doll. How can I convert it to a pattern for a pair of bloomers with a drawstring at the knees? The pattern I have is designed to have a waistband.

A
1. Most commercial patterns for drawers have a length well below the knees. Measure your doll from the waist to the knees along the side. This measurement would be **C-K** on your doll's Charlotte's Strip (waist **C** to knees **K**).

2. On the commercial pattern, measure **C-K** from the center of the waistline **C** stitching line down to the end of **K**, making a large pencil dot. Do not include the waist seam allowance in this measurement.

3. From the bottom edge of the commercial pattern, measure up to the large pencil dot at **K** in several places. Firmly fold the commercial pattern up along these marks. This is the **K** (knee) edge of the commercial pattern.

From here, you will start to convert the drawers to bloomers. You will need some clean paper, a ruler, measuring tape, a pencil, a pen, and scissors. Remember, my line drawings may appear not to scale and will look a bit strange. This is done purposely for clarity.

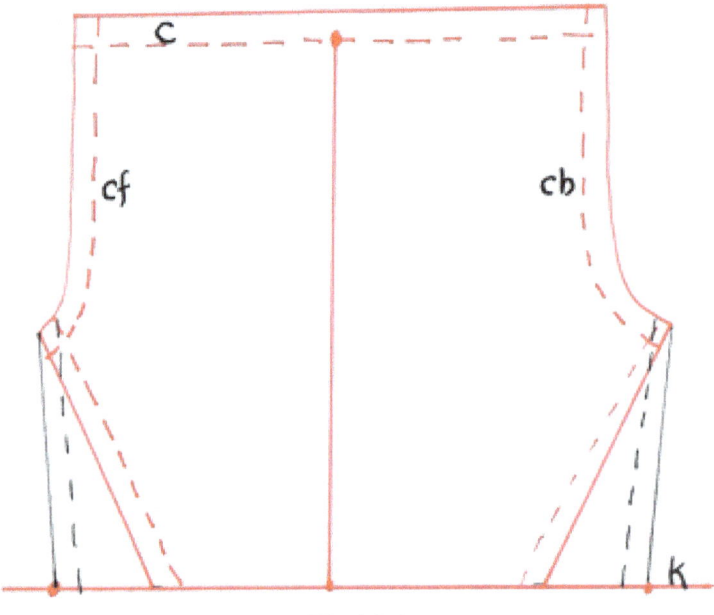

Fig.14-1

4. Measure 3 inches (8cm) upward along the lower edge of a piece of paper, making little pencil marks at each measurement. The paper must be large enough to accommodate your commercial pattern with at least 3 inches of space at the bottom edge. Draw a solid pencil line over these marks. This is now considered the **K** line. *(Fig.14-1)*

5. Place the folded bottom **K** edge of the commercial pattern along the **K** line. Trace a solid pencil outline of the pattern onto the paper and set the commercial pattern aside. Mark the tracing with the seam allowances found on the commercial pattern, adding **cf** to the front edge and **cb** to the back edge. Finally, mark the waistline as **C**. *(Fig.14-1)*

OK so far?

Now, let's begin making a drawstring closure at the knees. As with most commercial patterns, the inner leg lines slant inward. They are not going to give the bloomers a nice fullness at the knees. Thus, you need to straighten them out a bit.

6. From the center of the traced waistline seam stitching line **C**, draw a vertical pencil line downward to the **K** Line. *(Fig.14-1)*

7. Measure the width of the folded edge of the commercial pattern and add the amount of fullness you want.

8. Working along the **K** line, center your desired fullness measurement on the vertical **C-K** line, making a large pen dot at each end. Draw a solid pen line from the ends of the front and back

crotch down to these large pen dots. These are your new inner leg seam lines. Using the commercial pattern seam allowance, add seam allowances to the new inner leg edges. *(Fig.14-1)*

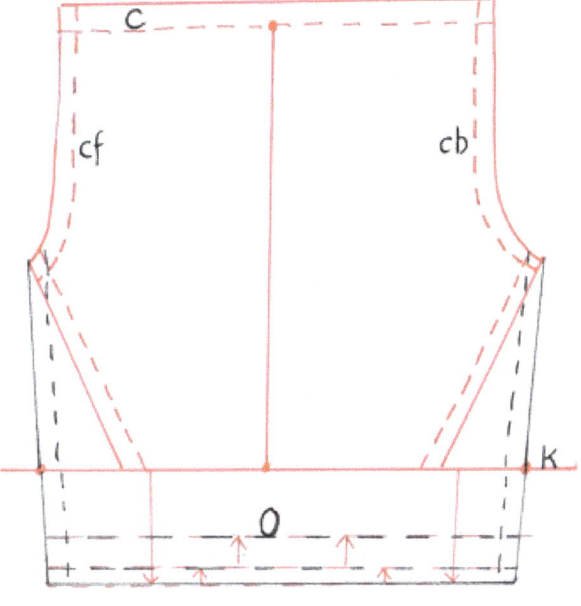

Fig.14-2

9. Most drawstring casings for dolls are 1/4 inch (6mm) wide. Measure 1 inch (3cm) downward from and along the **K** line, making little pencil marks at each measurement. Draw a solid pen line over these pencil marks. Extend the front and back inner leg edges to this solid line. *(Fig.14-2)*

10. Measure 1/8 inch (3mm) upward from and across the solid line, making little pencil marks at each measurement. Draw a broken pen line over these marks. From this 1/8-inch line, measure 1/4 inch upward from and across the broken line, making little pencil marks at each measurement. Draw a broken pen line over these marks. These two broken lines are the fold lines for the 1/4-inch drawstring casing. *(Fig.14-2)*

11. In the center of the casing, just above the 1/4-inch broken line, make a large "**0**." This is where you will create an opening for the drawstring. Besides adding enough length for the 1/4-inch drawstring casing, you have added 5/8 inch (2cm) to the length of the bloomers for a nice blousy effect around the doll's knees.

Cut out your new bloomers pattern and sew away.

KNEE CUFF
If you prefer a cuff at the knees instead of a drawstring, and if you are using a commercial drawers pattern and have prepared a tracing as described above (up to Step # 8, *Fig.14-1*), read on.

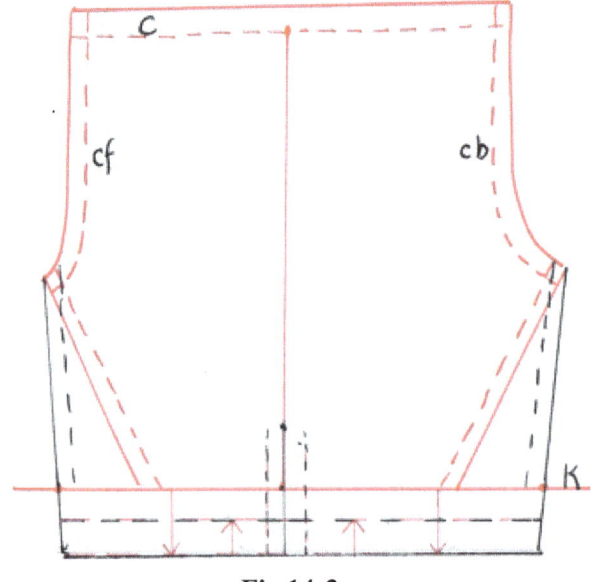

Fig.14-3

1. Measure 7/8 inch (2cm) downward from and along the **K** line, making little pencil marks at each measurement. Extend the front and back inner leg edges to these marks and draw a solid pen line over the pencil marks, connecting the front and back inner leg edges. *(Fig.14-3)*

2. Measure 1/4 inch (6mm) upward from and along this solid line, making little pencil marks at each measurement. Draw a broken pen line over these marks. You have included a 1/4-inch seam allowance plus a 5/8-inch (2cm) additional length for a nice blousy effect at the knees. *(Fig.14-3)*

3. Find the center of the bottom solid line and make a pencil mark. Draw a 1-inch (3cm) solid pen line upward from the solid line at this pencil mark. *(Fig.14-3)*

4. From each side of this solid pen line, measure 3/16 inch (5mm) outward, making little pencil marks. Draw broken pen lines through these pencil marks. You have created a 1-inch placket opening for a cuff with 3/16-inch seam allowances on each side of the opening. *(Fig.14-3)*

Cut out your new paper pattern for your doll's Bloomers with Cuffs at the knees.

Most plackets are 1/4 inch (6mm) wide. For the placket, you will need a piece of fabric twice the length of the placket opening and 7/8 inch wide. This width includes enough for the double 1/4-inch placket and the 3/16-inch seam allowance along each edge of the placket.

For the cuff, you will need the piece of fabric to match the width around your doll's knees (found on your doll's strip), as well as an extra inch. The will give the cuff a 3/16-inch seam allowance and a 1/4-inch overlap at each end.

Underwear Terms
Here are a few points of interest relating to a doll's underwear that you might find intriguing:

Breeches
Breeches are a two-legged garment, extending from the waist to just below the knees, worn fashionably by men from the late 16th to the early 19th centuries. The early style was full through the hips and tapered to below the knees. By the early 17th century, breeches were very full, ballooning from the waist to just above the knees. They were often decorated with pinking and slashing and had a visible center front opening.

By the 1620s, breeches were cut longer and slimmer, though still baggy around the hips, with a very wide waistband. By the late 17th century, their cut was altered so that, although still generous in the seat, the legs became more streamlined to fit under the long coat and waistcoat. By the mid-18th century, the center front opening was replaced with a flap-front opening. Depending on the width of the flap, the opening was known as a "small fall" or a "whole fall." Around this time, breeches became more tailored to fit the thighs more closely and fastened at the knee with buttons or a buckle.

By the end of the 18th century, breeches became longer and slimmer, bringing them closer to pantaloons. For a short time, they coexisted with pantaloons and trousers in fashionable circles but were gradually replaced by trousers. Breeches continued to be worn only as a court dress. Women have worn breeches since the late 19th century as part of sporting dress, especially under riding habits.

Briefs
This term has been used since the 1950s for both men's and women's figure-hugging underpants without legs. They are also referred to as pants or panties.

Drawers
An undergarment for the lower half of the torso and the legs, drawers are venerable garments designed to protect outer garments from bodily dirt. First worn by men, they were known as breeches or brais in the Middle Ages. Traditionally made of linen, they, along with the shirt, constituted a man's "linen." Drawers made of wool for men were also worn during the winter season. Drawers were made in a variety of lengths to suit fashion, the season, and the wearer. Ankle-length and knee-length were common in the 19th century. By the late 19th century, a distinction was made between knee-length drawers and ankle-length pants, known in everyday terms as "long johns."

Women began to wear drawers near the end of the 18th century. They were first made of cotton and were initially constructed like men's drawers, with a back-lacing waistband and fastened at the knees by an undecorated band. They were not commonly worn until the 1840s, by which time they resembled two long tubes connected only at the waistband. By the end of the 19th century, the knee-length drawers, unchanged in style, were highly decorated with frills, tucks, lace, etc., and the legs had widened. By the early 1900s, the word "knickers" had become the preferred term even for women's open-legged drawers, which were, in any case, passing out of fashion. The word drawers became the standard term used by costume specialists to categorize undergarments.

Knickerbockers
These are a kind of breeches with baggy legs that hung slightly over bands fastened below the knees. They have been worn by men and boys since the mid-1800s, usually with long thick hose pulled up over the lower part of the knee band along with ankle boots or lace-up shoes. Boys wore knickerbocker suits with the breeches either open or closed at the knees. Men adopted them as part of a shooting or country dress and, much later, golfing attire. Women's knickerbockers appeared as undergarment-like drawers with a closed crotch and legs fastened with buttons or elastic around the knees. They gradually became feminine sporting attire.

Knickers
These refer to a pair of women's closed drawers. The term has been used since 1880 and is a shortened form of knickerbocker. The name caught on quickly, and by the end of the century, even open-legged drawers were being referred to as knickers. Once open-legged drawers began to pass out of fashion early in the 1900s, the words "drawers" and "knickers" began to be used interchangeably.

The more feminine and attractive knickers were made with wide frilly legs. Another popular style, more related to the original knickerbockers, featured buttoned knee-length legs. Some even had buttoned back-flaps. By the second decade of the 1900s, knee-length knickers with elastic at the leg openings were called directoire knickers and remained popular from the 1920s through the 1940s, when they were made from either woven or lock-knit fabrics. French knickers had wide legs and reached the upper and mid-thigh. By the 1950s, most knickers did not have any legs at all and could also be referred to as "pants" or "briefs."

Pantaloons
These were a man's fashionably tight-fitting garment for the hips and legs. They were worn from the 1790s to the 19th century, and varied in form from period to period. The legs descended to mid-calf or mid-ankle and were usually tied or buttoned at the ends. The desired close fit depended on the elasticity of the material used to make them, which was either knitted jersey, bias-cut cloth, or some soft, supple leather. The introduction of pantaloons into the world of fashion was a logical transition between increasingly tighter knee-breeches and trousers. They appealed to the tastes of the time by displaying the masculine body. Pale colors were popular at first, with black becoming more prevalent as time went on. By the 1830s, black was the only color permissible in fashionable circles. Pantaloons were not part of women's attire.

Bloomers
Women's baggy underpants fastened just below or above the knee are also known as "bloomers" (or "knickers" or "directoire knickers"). They were most popular from 1910 to the 1930s but continued to be worn by older women for several decades thereafter. Often, the term *bloomers* has

been used interchangeably with the pantalettes worn by women and girls in the mid-19th century and the open-leg knee-length drawers of the late 19th and early 20th centuries.

Pantalettes

Pantalettes are undergarments covering the legs, worn by women, girls, and very young boys in the early- to mid-19th century. They originated in France in the early 19th century and quickly spread to Britain and America. They were a form of leggings or long drawers and could be one-piece or two separate garments—one for each leg—attached at the waist with buttons or laces. The crotch was left open for hygiene reasons. They were most often made of white linen fabric and could be decorated with tucks, lace, cutwork, or *Broderie Anglaise*.

Ankle-length pantalettes for women were worn under the crinoline and hoop skirt to ensure that the legs were modestly covered should they become exposed. Pantalettes for children and young girls were mid-calf to ankle-length and were intended to show under their shorter skirts. Until the mid-19th century, very young boys were commonly dressed in dresses, gowns, and pantalettes, though these were generally associated with girls' clothing, until the boys were breeched at any age between two and eight years, and sometimes older. Young boys would be dressed in this fashion until they were at least toilet-trained.

Think I'll stay with drawers or bloomers for girl dolls. Boy dolls get knee-length pantalettes or knickerbockers for their underwear. But no dresses!

Sleeves

Drawstring at Wrist

Q
How do I make a blouse full-sleeve pattern with gathers in the cap and at the wrists for my doll? I only have a rather plain tapered sleeve pattern. Also, I am not sure how to make a drawstring casing at the wrists or how to add a cuff. Additionally, how would I make a gathered edge trimmed with lace at the wrists?

A
Making a full-sleeve pattern using your tapered pattern is the easy part. Adding length for a drawstring casing or a cuff is another matter—a bit more complicated, but not too hard to figure out.

You will need some clean paper, a ruler, measuring tape, a pencil, a pen, and scissors. Your pattern must also be free of wrinkles. A warm iron can fix that problem. If the line drawings (Fig.) are not to scale, this is purposely done for clarity.

1. There is usually a mark in the sleeve cap that indicates where the cap should be placed in the armscye to align it with the shoulder seam. I call this mark **S** for shoulder. It usually sits away

from the center of the sleeve cap and slightly toward the back of the sleeve. Make a large pen mark over this mark on your pattern, marking as **S**. Draw a vertical pen line from **S** to the wrist edge (**W** for wrist).

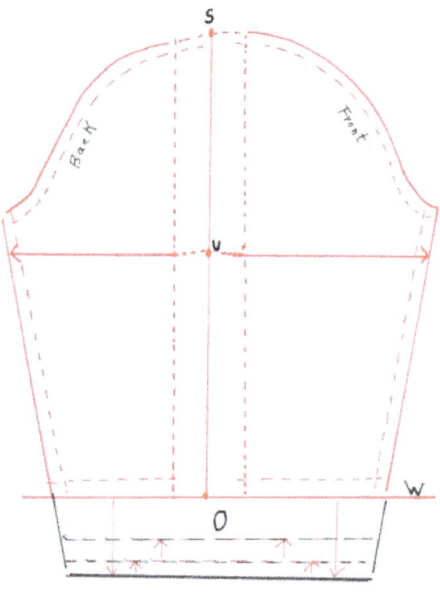

Fig.15-1

2. Draw a pencil line 2 inches (5cm) up from and along the bottom edge of a clean piece of paper. The paper should be large enough to accommodate your pattern. Mark this line as **W**.

3. Place the wrist edge of the pattern along the penciled line on the paper. Make a large pencil dot **S** on the paper. Remove the pattern. Draw a vertical pencil line from **S** down to the **W** line on the paper. *(Fig.15-1)*

4. Find the **S-U** (shoulder **S** to mid-upper arm **U**) measurement on your doll's Charlotte Strip. Transfer this measurement on the **S-W** line, starting at **S**, making a large pencil dot at the end of the **S-U** measurement. Label the dot **U**. *(Fig.15-1)*

5. Fold your pattern along the penciled **S-W** line and cut it along the fold. It can be taped back together again, but you need two parts here. You will notice that the back of the sleeve pattern is a bit narrower than the front, which is OK. Remember, **S** is slightly toward the back of the sleeve cap, not in the center.

6. Place the wrist edge of the two parts along the **W** line on the paper, spacing them apart just enough to accommodate the fullness you want. The fullness measurement should be from the front underarm seam stitching line to the back underarm stitching line, at the **U** level (arrows), and not within the space between the two parts. The two parts should be equidistant from the **S-W** line. *(Fig.15-1)*

7. Trace a solid pencil line around the pattern pieces, connecting the two along the top edge. Remove the two parts and set them aside. Mark the tracing with all the marks found on the pattern, including all seam allowances. *(Fig.15-1)*

   You now have a sleeve pattern full enough for gathers in the cap. Let's work on the wrist end.

8. Measure 1 inch (3cm) downward from and along the **W** line, making small pencil marks at each measurement. Extend the front and back underarm edges to these pencil marks and draw a solid pen line over them, connecting the underarm edges. *(Fig.15-1)*

9. Measure 1/8 inch (3mm) upward from and along the solid line, making little pencil marks at each measurement. Draw a broken pen line over these marks.

10. Measure 1/4 inch (6mm) upward from and along the 1/8-inch line, making little pencil marks. Draw a broken pen line over these marks. These two broken lines are the fold lines of the wrist drawstring casing. *(Fig.15-1)*

11. Find the center of the casing, just above the 1/4-inch line, and draw an "**0**." This is the opening through which a drawstring is inserted. *(Fig.15-1)*

    You have added enough length to the sleeve for a 1/4-inch drawstring casing, as well as 5/8 inch (2cm) of additional length for a nice blousy effect over the wrist.

CUFF AT WRIST

For a full sleeve with a cuff at the wrists, follow the steps above up to the point where you add enough for the drawstring casing, Step #7, Fig.15-1.

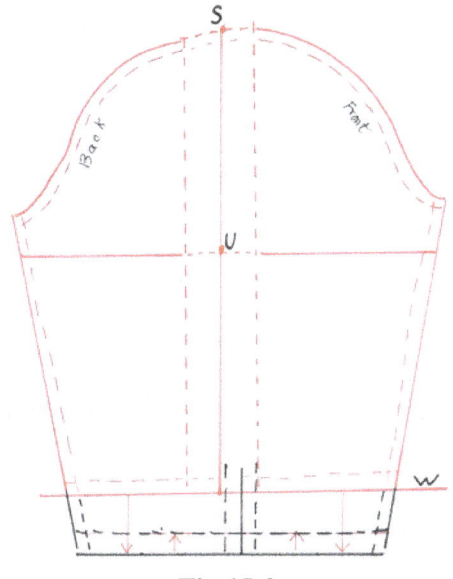

Fig.15-2

1. Measure 5/8 inch (2cm) downward from and along the **W** line, making little pencil marks at each measurement. Extend the front and back underarm edges to these marks and draw a solid pen line over the pencil marks, connecting the front and back underarm edges. *(Fig.15-2)*

2. Measure 1/4 inch (6mm) upward from and along the solid line, making little pencil marks at each measurement. Draw a broken pen line over these marks. You have included a 1/4-inch seam allowance plus an extra 3/4 inch (2cm) for a nice blousy effect over the wrist. *(Fig.5-2)*

3. Find the center of the bottom solid line and make a pencil mark. Draw a 1-inch (3cm) solid pen line upward from the pencil mark. *(Fig.15-2)*

4. From each side of this pen line, measure 3/16 inch (5mm) outward, making little pencil marks at each measurement. Draw broken pen lines through these pencil marks with the pen. You have made a 1-inch placket opening for a cuff in the sleeve pattern with 3/16-inch seam allowances. *(Fig.15-2)*

For the placket, you will need a piece of fabric twice the length of the placket opening and 7/8 inch (2cm) wide. The width includes enough for the double 1/4-inch placket plus the 3/16-inch seam allowance along each edge of the placket.

For the cuff, you will need the piece of fabric to match the width around your doll's wrist **W** (found on your doll's Charlotte Strip), as well as 1–7/8 inches (5cm). The extra length includes a 3/16-inch seam allowance and a 1/4-inch overlap at each end.

Lace to Wrist
To add lace to the full wrist edge, follow the directions above up to where you add length for either a drawstring casing or a cuff, Step #7, *Fig.15-1*.

1. Measure 5/8 inch (2cm) downward from the **W** line, making little pencil marks at each measurement. Extend the underarm seam edges down to the pencil marks and draw a solid pen line over these marks, connecting the underarm seam edges. This is the new wrist W edge.

2. When a sleeve has been cut out, place the lace along the wrist edge, matching the edge of the lace to the wrist edge. Sew the lace to the sleeve, stitching in the lace heading. Cut away the extra fabric under the lace.

3. Weave some narrow ribbon through the lace heading. When pulled, the ribbon gathers the sleeve edge around the doll's wrists. Also, the added 5/8 inch will give the sleeve a nice blousy effect over the doll's wrists.

There you are. You now know several different ways to treat the wrist end of full sleeves.

FULL CAP

Q

How do I make a blouse sleeve pattern for my doll with gathers only in the cap? The pattern I have is for a plain tapered sleeve.

A

This is not too hard. You will need some clean paper, a ruler, a pencil, a pen, and scissors. Ensure the pattern piece is free of wrinkles; a warm iron can help with this.

There usually is a mark in the sleeve cap that represents the placement of the cap into the armscye, matching this mark with the shoulder seam of the armscye. I named this mark **S** (shoulder). It is typically slightly off-center toward the back of the cap. Make a large pencil dot over this mark on your pattern and mark it **S**.

1. Using the ruler, draw a pencil line connecting the ends of the armscye curve (at the sleeve underarm seam lines) across the pattern. Cut the pattern along this line. Trust me here—if you are uncomfortable directly cutting up a pattern, make a tracing of the pattern on a clean piece of paper and use the tracing instead.

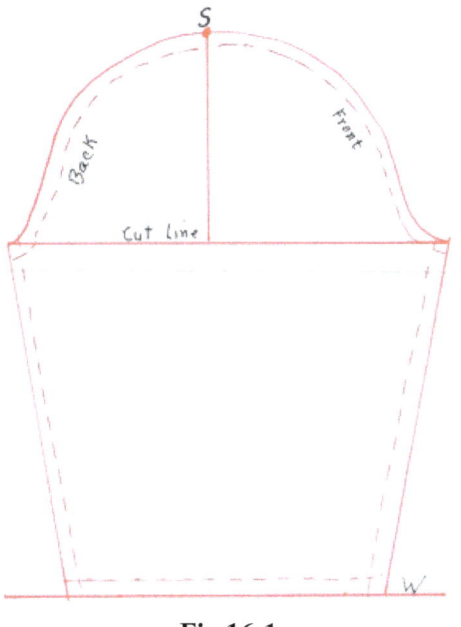

Fig.16-1

2. Draw a 1 inch (3cm) pencil line upward from and along the bottom edge of a clean piece of paper. Label it **W**. Place the wrist edge of the bottom part of the pattern on this line.

3. Trace a solid pencil line around the outer edges of this piece of the pattern. Remove the pattern and set it aside. Mark the seam allowances on this part of the pattern. *(Fig.16-1)*

93

4. Position the cap piece against the top of the tracing. With the pen, mark **S** on the paper. Remove the cap piece. Draw a vertical pencil line downward from **S** to the top edge of the traced bottom piece. This will be the **S** line. *(Fig.16-1)*

5. Fold the cap piece over at **S** matching the cut edges in the fold. Cut the piece along the fold. The back part will appear slightly narrower than the front part. This is OK. Remember, **S** is a little off-center of the cap.

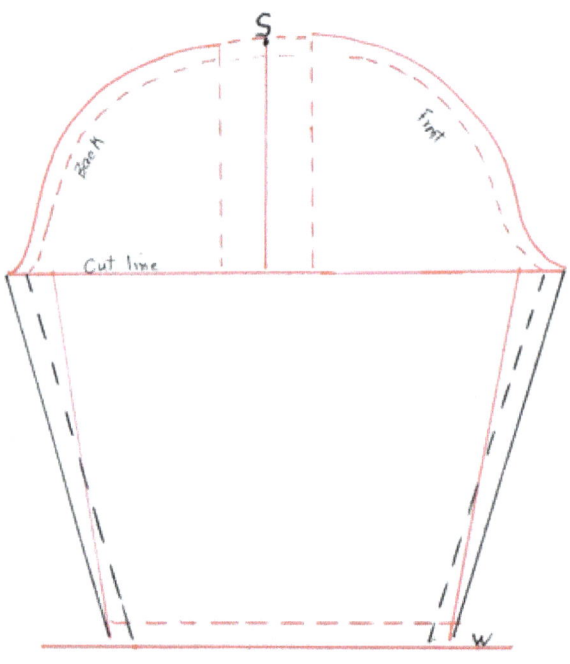

Fig.16.2

6. Decide how full you want the sleeve cap to be. Position the two parts of the cap pattern against the top of the tracing, spacing them apart enough for your measurement to be from the front armscye edge to the back armscye edge (not within the space between the two parts). The front and back pieces should be equidistant from the **S** line. *(Fig.16-2)*

7. Trace a solid pencil outline of the new cap, connecting the two pieces along the top of the cap. Set the two parts aside. *(Fig.16-2)*

8. Starting at each armscye end of the new cap, draw a solid pen line on each side of the sleeve tracing to the **W** line. These are the new underarm seam edges. Mark these edges with the underarm seam allowances of the pattern. *(Fig.16-2)*

You now have your blouse sleeve pattern with fullness only in the cap.

ABOUT SLEEVE PATTERNS

Never add fullness to a sleeve by adding width to the front and back underarm edges. Instead, cut a sleeve pattern apart along an **S** line, top to bottom, spacing the two parts to the desired width, and proceed from there. The desired width should not be within the space between the two parts. Rather it should include the width of the two parts and the space between, measured from the front underarm seam stitching line to the back underarm seam stitching line (excluding seam allowances), and through the upper arm level.

If you want longer sleeves, don't add to the wrist edge. Instead, cut your pattern apart across the upper arm area, space the two pieces to the desired extra length, and go from there. Again, the extra length should not be the space within the two parts. Rather, it should include the length of each part and the space between, measured from the cap seam stitching line to the wrist seam stitching line (excluding seam allowances).

If you want a sleeve to fit a shorter arm, cut your pattern across the upper arm area, and overlap the cut edges until you attain the desired length from the cap seam stitching line to the wrist edge stitching line (excluding seam allowances).

If you just want shorter sleeves with no wrist edges, measure down the arm from the doll's shoulder to where you want the sleeve to fall. Measure your sleeve pattern down from the center top of the sleeve cap's seam line to this same measurement. Add a new 1/4-inch (6mm) seam allowance if you are adding a cuff. Alternatively, add enough for a hem and cut the pattern away at these measurements.

NECKLINES

Too Tight

Q
I just completed a dress for my doll, following the directions regarding the pattern. But to my dismay, I discovered that the neckline was too tight around the doll's neck. What can I do? I used some very nice fabric for the dress, and I just hate the thought of tossing it aside. The bodice of the dress is lined, and it seems almost impossible to get inside to make the neckline wider without taking the whole dress apart. I'm at my wit's end! Help!

A
Oh dear! I've been there myself. Here's what to do:

1. First, using a small pair of very sharp scissors, carefully snip a stitching thread in the neck seam. Then, ever so carefully, using a thin straight pin, carefully pick all the thread from this seam around the neck edge. I am assuming that the little dress opens in the back.

2. Pop out the bodice and lining seam edges and pin them together, treating them as one layer. Baste the edges together, about 1/8 inch (3mm) below the original stitching line using small stitches. Trim the original two-layered seam allowance away, cutting along the original stitching line. The two layers of the new neck edge will be considered as one layer with the 1/8-inch row of stitches still in place.

3. Measure the length of the new neck edge and cut a bias piece from the fabric you used for the dress. This should be 1 inch (3cm) wide and 1 inch longer than your measurement.

4. Press the bias strip into a curved shape about the same size as the dress's neckline.

5. Starting at the center back, with the right sides together, pin the inside curve of the bias strip to the neck edge, adjusting the fit of the bias. Remember to leave the ends sticking out from the back edges.

6. Baste the bias strip and neck edge together, along your first line of 1/8-inch stitches. Remove the pins. Using a fabric marker, draw a new 3/16-inch (5mm) stitching line around the neck edge. This will make it easier to sew the new neck seam. Stitch the new seam, then remove the basting threads and snip the new seam allowance just until the seam stitches.

Still with me?

7. Finger-press the bias strip along the stitched seam (up and away from the neckline). Hand-sew a line of very small stitches through the three layers around the neckline, on the bias strip side, close to the seam stitches.

8. Fold the free edge of the bias strip under about 1/8 inch, finger-pressing the fold in place. Fold the bias strip over to the inside of the bodice and finger-press the turned edge. You might want to baste the turned edge to keep it neatly turned while you finish placing the bias strip in place.

9. Pin the bias to the inside of the neck edge, adjusting the fit of the bias strip around the neck edge. Trim the free ends of the bias strip at the back edge to 1/4 inch (6mm) and fold them under the bias strip. Pin it in place along the back edge. Tack these edges in place and remove the pins.

10. Blind stitch the folded edge of the bias strip to the bodice lining only. You don't want these stitches to be visible on the outside of the bodice.

There you are. Hey! You really did all this on purpose, right? A little slightly gathered narrow lace might be a dainty touch to the neckline. Maybe use the same lace trim you've used to decorate the dress to "tie" the two together.

Too Large

Q

Carefully, or so I thought, I measured my doll and made a pattern for a dress. I wanted it to be perfect, as I intended to enter my doll into a competition. To my dismay, after completing the construction of the dress bodice, including the lining and set-in sleeves, the neckline was too wide! What can I do without having to remake the entire bodice? The fabric I used was quite expensive, and the thought of making another bodice is stressful.

A

Dare I say that we've all been here, but don't despair. There is an easy way to solve this problem: attach a gathered piece of lace to the neckline. The lace can be slightly wider than any other lace on the dress. If you haven't used any lace trim on the dress, make sure this lace is special. The lace should be wide enough to cover the space left by the too-wide neckline of your doll's dress.

1. Measure around the bodice neckline and cut a piece of lace one and a half times this length.

2. Hem each end and pull up one of the gathering threads in the lace heading to fit the lace around the bodice neckline. Pin the lace in place, adjust the gathers evenly around the neckline, and whipstitch the heading to the neckline.

3. Weave the ends of the gathering thread back into your stitches for about 1/2 inch and trim away the threads. Gently tug on the lace to make it lie in a gentle ruffle that lies flat around the bodice neckline. A little steam from the iron will set the lace in place nicely.

You may wish to use the same lace somewhere else on the dress to tie the design together, making it look as if you had planned it that way.

Cotton-knit Socks

Q

I've seen dolls wearing nice-looking cotton-knit socks that are hemmed and have a nice straight-back seam. Some have a colored woven band around the hem for decoration. I would like to make some for my dolls. How do I go about making a pattern for them?

A

A clean, white T-shirt will work nicely for the fabric of your doll's socks. Trim away all the seams and sewn hems, and you will have enough cotton-knit fabric for many pairs of doll socks. The strait of fabric, which you would use for the length of the socks, should follow the knit pattern, while the width should go across it. The right side is the knitted side, and the wrong side is the pearled side. You will also need some fusible web and a small Teflon sheet. To make a pattern, you will need some clean paper, a pair of scissors, a ruler, measuring tape, pencil, and pen.

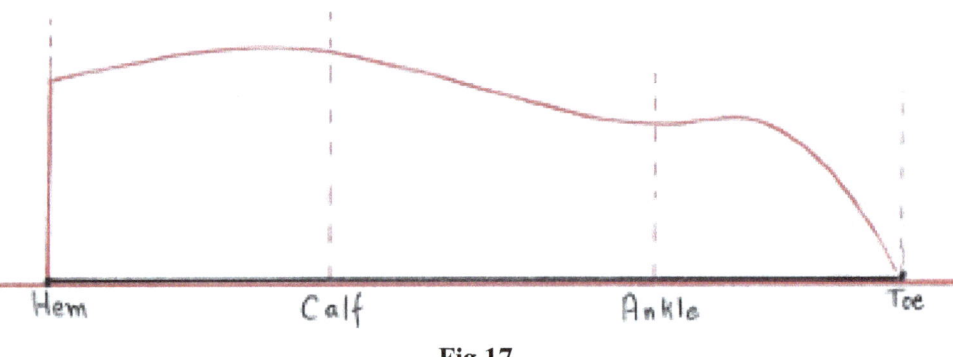

Fig.17

1. To make a sock pattern, measure from the toes, around the bottom of the foot, and the back of the heel, up to where you want the hem to be on the doll's leg. Add another 1/4 inch (6mm) for the top hem.

2. Draw a pencil line across the edge of a clean piece of paper about 2 inches (5cm) above the edge. Draw a pen line representing your sock measurement along this line, making dots where the toe and top of the sock fall on the line. *(Fig.17)*

3. Measure around the doll's calf and ankles. From the drawn pen line, make a pencil mark at half of these measurements at the calf and ankle area of the sock. Draw a curved pencil line from the top of the hem, around the calf (through the pencil mark), dipping into the ankle area, and around the bottom of the foot to the toe. If the first pattern doesn't seem to fit the doll, repeat these steps until you have a pattern you are satisfied with.

4. Cut out your sock pattern. Make a fabric marker 1/4-inch fold line at the top of the pattern for the 1/4-inch hem. *(Fig.17)*

5. Cut a piece of the knit fabric four times the widest part of the pattern plus 1/2 inch (on the right side and across the knit), and the length of the pattern plus 1/2 inch (on the right side and along the knit).

6. Place this piece on the ironing board, right side down. Cut a 1/4-inch wide strip of the fusible web, just long enough to fit along one long edge of the piece of cotton knit (on the wrong side and across the pearl of the fabric). Carefully, without dislodging the piece of fusible web, place the Teflon sheet over the fusible web and the cotton knit.

6. Place a warm iron directly on the Teflon sheet for a few seconds, just long enough to melt the fusible web onto the cotton knit. It will also stick to the Teflon sheet, but not to worry. When the Teflon sheet has cooled, gently peel the cotton knit.

7. Fold the edge with the fusible web 1/4 inch over to the wrong side. Press the folded edge with the warm iron for a few seconds, and there! You have a fused hem.

9. Cut the hemmed piece in half lengthwise. Further fold each half in half, right sides in. Place the straight edge of your sock pattern along the folded edge and the 1/4-inch fold line aligned with the hemmed top edge, then cut out the sock. Repeat for the second sock.

Zigzag the double back edge, backstitching over the hem and leaving a 1/2-inch tail of threads at the toe. Turn the sock right-side out. Neat?

You can decorate your socks as you please.

"A" Design Slip

Q
I would like to make an A-design slip for my 12-inch German doll. I have heard that one can use a natural waist slip bodice pattern to make an A-design slip, but I am not too sure as to how to do this. Please help.

A
These little slips are my favorite to make. You can do so much with them. I make lace panels in the front in circle, diamond, or triangle shapes. I sew several rows of machine embroidery (whitework) around the hem. Sometimes, I add a little ruffle or gathered lace along the hem. The neck and armhole edges can be finished with handmade scallops or trimmed with slightly gathered lace edging, or even both. Narrow-colored China silk ribbon bows make dainty touches. So, have some fun making your little A-shaped slip.

Making a pattern for an A-design slip using your natural waist slip bodice pattern is relatively easy. The only parts of the bodice pattern you will be using are the shoulder, neck, and armscye edges. You will need the slip bodice front and back pattern pieces, a few pieces of printer paper, a clear ruler, a pen, a pencil, a tape measure, and some tape. For your reference, in the illustrations (Fig.), pencil lines/dots/marks are made with **red** ink.

1. If the slip front bodice pattern is cut on the fold, you will need a full front pattern. Make a pencil tracing of the front pattern on a piece of paper. Make a mirror image of the tracing by placing the cut-on-fold edge of the pattern against the cut-on-fold edge of the tracing and trace it. There! You now have a full slip front bodice pattern to work with.

2. Draw a horizontal pencil line across the pattern, connecting the two armscye ends. Cut the pattern along this line. You only need the top part. If you are uncomfortable with cutting your pattern, make a tracing of it on a clean piece of paper and use it instead.

3. Place your new pattern piece at the top of a piece of paper. Make a pencil tracing of the shoulders, neck, and armscye edges. Mark the tracing with seam allowances. *(Fig.18-1)*

4. Connect the armpit ends of the armscyes with a horizontal pencil line and make a large pencil dot at each end. This is the Armscye Line. *(Fig.18-1)*

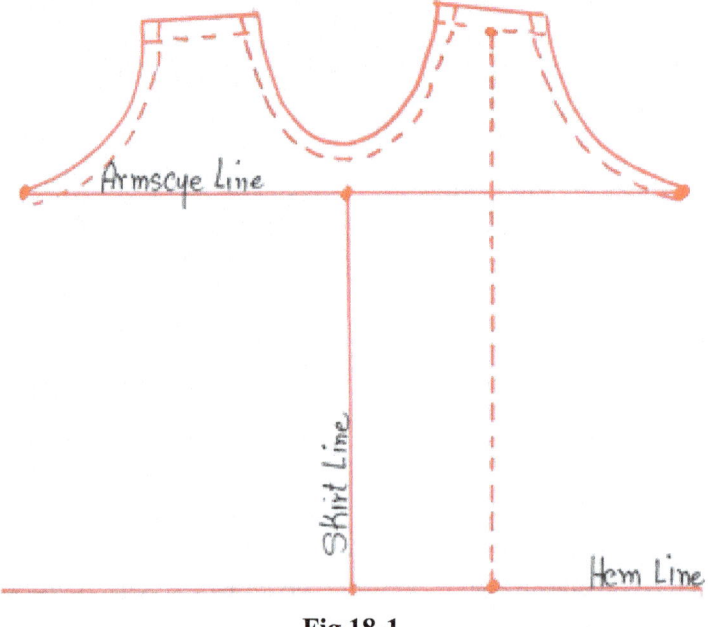

Fig.18-1

5. Measure your doll from the top center of one shoulder to where you want the slip hem to fall. Transfer this measurement to the tracing, working down from the seam stitching line of one shoulder tracing (no seam allowance is included in this measurement) to the end of the slip measurement and make a large pencil dot. Draw a broken pencil line along this measurement. *(Fig.18-1)*

6. Draw a horizontal pencil line through the large pencil dot across the paper. This is the Hem Line. *(Fig.18-1)*

7. Find the center of the Armscye Line and make a large pencil dot. From this dot, draw a solid vertical pencil line down to the Hem Line. This is the Skirt Line. *(Fig.18-1)*

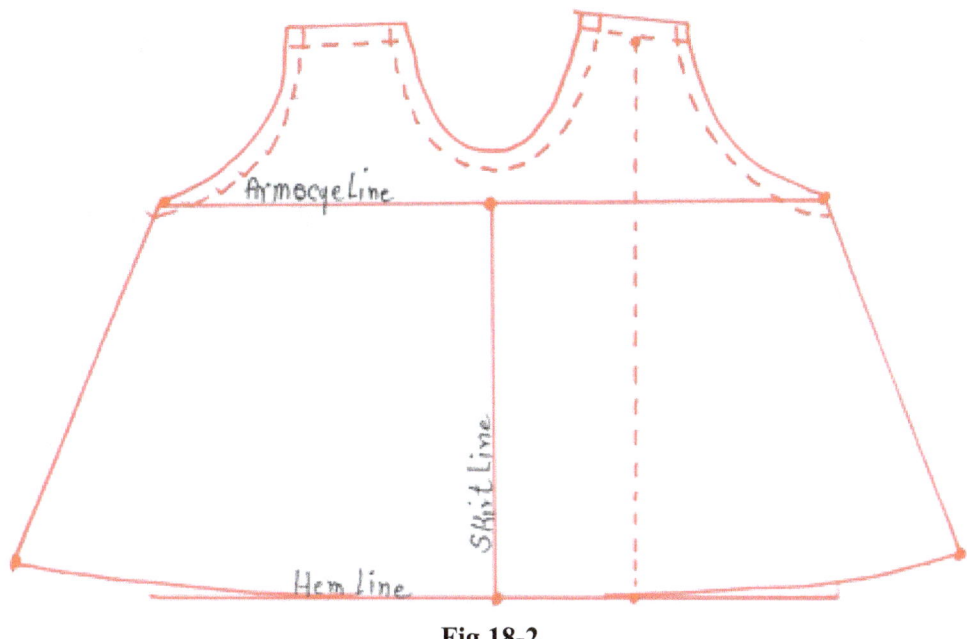

Fig.18-2

8. Measure the Skirt Line. Using this measurement, draw angled pencil lines extending them from the dots at the ends of the armscyes. Make large dots at the ends of these lines. The ends of these lines should be equal distance from the Skirt Line. These angled lines represent the side edges of the A-design slip.

9. From the large dots, draw gentle curved lines to the end of the Skirt Line at the Hem Line. Cut out your new A-Design Slip Front Pattern. *(Fig.18-2)*

The fullness of your A-design slip depends on how deep you make the angled side edges. The higher the angles, the fuller the slip. Another way to increase the fullness of an A-design slip without raising the level of the angled sides is to make small reverse box pleats at the center front neckline and at the underarm seams.

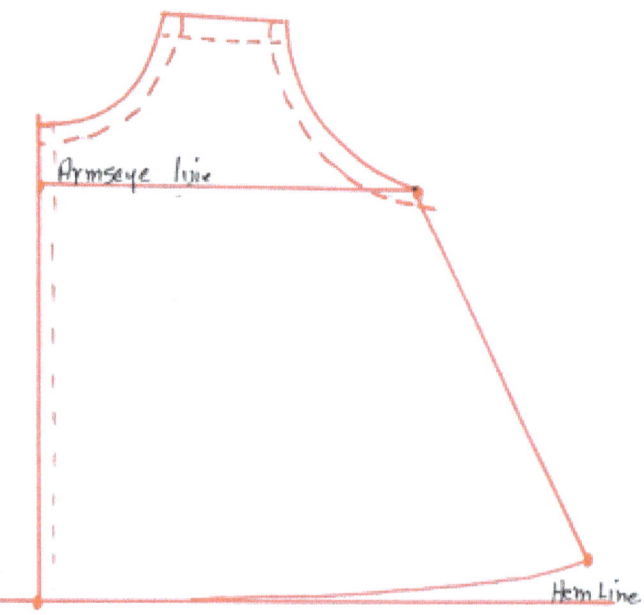

Fig.18-3

10. The slip-back bodice can be used similarly, except you don't need to make a mirror image. Draw a horizontal pencil line straight across the back pattern at the armscye end level.

11. Make a pencil tracing of the neck, shoulder, armscye, and back edges of your slip-back pattern onto a piece of paper. *(Fig.18-3)*

12. Place the corresponding part of the A-Design slip front pattern over the tracing, matching the armscye ends and the penciled horizontal lines. With the pencil, trace the skirt side and hem edges. There you have it—your new A-Design Slip Back Pattern.

On General Sewing

Note: If I include a line drawing or two for your reference, all pencil marks, lines, and arrows in a line drawing are represented by red ink. Fabric in a line drawing is represented by blue ink. Pen marks, lines, and digits are represented by black ink.

SEWING DEFINITIONS

Q
HELP! I am so confused. I am very new to sewing, and some of the terms I come across in sewing instructions are so strange: Cutting Line, Seam Line, Seam Allowance, Stitching Line, Underarm Seam, Running Stitch, Blanket Stitch, Buttonhole Stitch, Slipstitch, to name a few. And what is an Armscye? Is basting really important? Also, I read a direction somewhere to mark all cut-on-fold edges with red ink. Why?

A
Ah, dear novice, I'll do my best to relieve your confusion by providing definitions of the terms causing your concern. So, relax and read on.

CUTTING LINE
This is the very outside edge of a pattern piece that you cut along when you cut out a paper pattern. Or it may be a line that the pattern instructions direct you to cut.

SEAMLINE
This is usually the broken line on a pattern along which you stitch two pieces of a garment together. Sometimes, a pattern does not have these lines, and you must mark them yourself. No big deal. This is also called the Stitching Line. It may also be a line that the pattern instructions direct you to stitch.

SEAM ALLOWANCE
This is the width of the seam. Most pattern pieces for us big people have a 5/8-inch (2cm) seam allowance. Most doll patterns have 3/16- to 1/4-inch (5mm to 6mm) seam allowances. Get the

picture? If you are basting pieces of a garment together, it is always advisable to baste within the seam allowance. Then the basting threads are easy to remove after stitching a seam.

UNDERARM SEAM

This is the seam in a sleeve that is under the arm.

RUNNING STITCH

This is a basting stitch, but it is most often used to hand-sew seams together, as with garments for tiny dolls, or when one wishes to hand-sew a garment. It is called a running stitch because the needle passes (runs) through the fabric, back and forth, for long sections at a time without being withdrawn from the fabric. The sewing thread follows the needle through the fabric. *(Fig.19)*

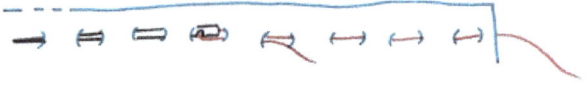

Fig.19

BLANKET STITCH

This can serve both decorative and functional purposes. You can use it as a decorative edge trim or as an overcast on raw seams. They are evenly spaced and evenly stitched, though, as a decoration, the length of the stitches can vary. For example, one long, one short. The needle is inserted off the edge to be trimmed and over the thread. *(Fig.20)*

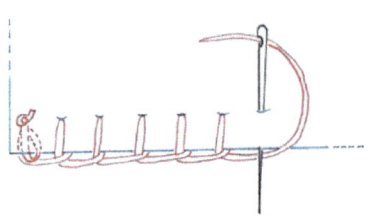

Fig.20

BUTTONHOLE STITCH

This is a variation of the blanket stitch. Although often mistaken for a closely done blanket stitch, it is slightly different. The buttonhole stitch is a knotted blanket stitch. To make this stitch, work along the edge by inserting the needle into the edge and through a loop, then pull the thread to make a knot. *(Fig.21-1)*

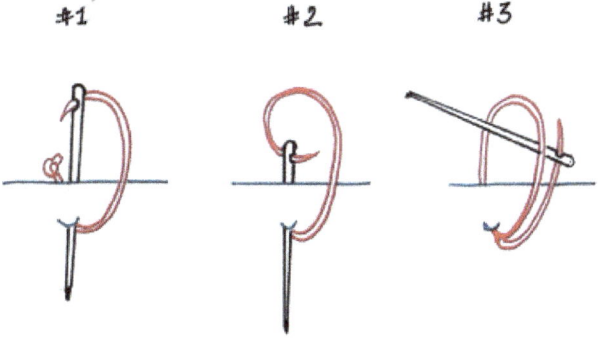

Fig.21-1

#1 – Insert your needle into the backside of the buttonhole edge, pulling the thread up until the knot touches the fabric.
#2 – Make another stitch in the same place, leaving a loop of the double thread.
#3 – Make another stitch in the same place, this time passing the needle through the back of the loop, pulling the threads up tight and making a knot at the buttonhole edge (**#4**).
These first three (3) steps are the beginning of the buttonhole stitch.

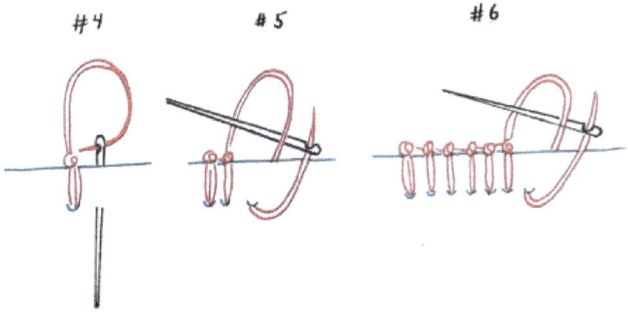

Fig.21-2

#4 – Make another stitch next to the knotted stitch, leaving a loop (as in **#2** above).
#5 – Pass the needle through the back of the loop, pulling the threads together tightly and making a knot at the buttonhole edge.
#6 – Continue stitching in this manner, following **#4** and **#5**, making closely stitched buttonhole stitches all around the buttonhole edge. *(Fig.21-2)*

SLIPSTITCH

This is that magic stitch that can make your stitching look invisible on both the right side and the wrong side while effectively joining fabric. For dolls, it is mostly used to sew various hems in place. *(Fig.22)*

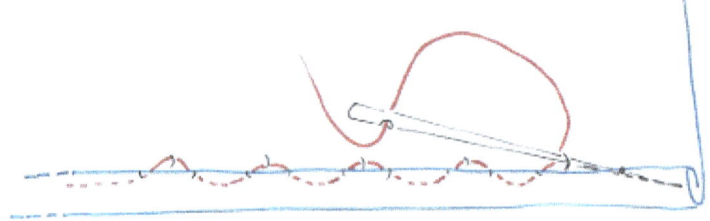

Fig.22

BACK STITCH

One can easily confuse back stitching with a back stitch. Back stitching is a sewing machine stitch used to secure the beginning or end of a seam, preventing the seam from opening unnecessarily at either end. A back stitch is used in hand sewing, especially for seams under strain, like an armscye. *(Fig.23)*

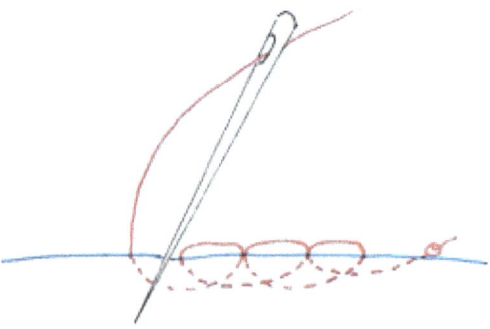

Fig.23

ARMSCYE

This is another name for an armhole. It's an archaic dressmaker's term, but more fashionable than plain "armhole." Don't you think?

MARK CUT-ON-FOLD LINES RED

The reason I instruct sewers to mark all cut-on-folds with red ink is that, often, someone will overlook the instructions on a pattern and cut out two pieces instead of one on a fold. Sometimes, a pattern piece has two edges to be placed on folds. The red ink serves as a red flag to remember!

BASTING

Basting is very important, especially for the novice sewer. Even after years of sewing, I still baste. Basting holds together two pieces that are being sewn until the process is complete. Yes, one can use pins instead, but then the edges that are meant to be kept together while sewing can become skewed and don't match. The result is uneven seams or one edge ending up shorter than the other. So, do baste. Another reason for basting is when you are using thin or silk fabrics, the basting threads keep the fabric stable as it passes under the machine's feed dogs, giving the needle something stable to stitch into. Of course, these basting threads are not meant to be removed, so one has to be careful of stitching over them.

Sewing Machine Needles

Type

Q

Selecting the right sewing machine needle for various sewing tasks is confusing. What type of needle should I use for sewing knit fabrics, and why?

A

There are three kinds of sewing machine needles that I can think of off the top of my head. When sewing with woven fabrics, a sharply pointed sewing machine needle is used. The size of the needle depends on the weight of the fabric. The sharp points of the needles cut through the fabrics without harming them. If you look closely at a piece of fabric that has been sewn with a sharp needle under a microscope, you will see where the needle has broken parts of the woven threads, entered, and exited the fabric. This causes no harm to the garment, however.

Sewing with knitted fabrics is another matter; when you tear or break a thread in knitted fabric, you might cause a ladder (run), so you wouldn't want to use a regular sharp-pointed sewing machine needle. The nicely rounded ends of the special needles for knitted fabrics pass through the fabric, parting the fabric threads without cutting or tearing them. You would also use a slightly longer stitch length.

When sewing with leather, you shouldn't use the same machine needles as for woven fabrics. Regular needles often stick in the leather, preventing a stitch from being completed. There are specific needles designed for leather, featuring sharp points with knife-like edges that cut through the leather effectively. You can see these unique points under a microscope. Similarly, stitches viewed under a microscope reveal tiny, minuscule cuts next to the thread, which do not damage the leather.

Snagging

Q

I am having a terrible time with my sewing machine needle. It keeps snagging in the fabric that I am using to make some underwear for my dolls. What is happening?

A

Sewing machine needles don't last forever. Just because one looks straight in the machine doesn't mean it is or that the point is still sharp. Your problem could be due to the needle's point becoming blunt or bent—a burr. The needle may have hit a pin or simply worn down from overuse.

If you sew frequently, you should change your needles often. Ideally, use a new needle for each new sewing project. Needles become blunt from repeatedly piercing fabric and can also bend slightly from hitting pins, though this may be too minuscule to see without a magnifying glass.

The size of the needle you use is crucial for different projects. For fine, lightweight fabrics like batiste, muslin, silk, or silk brocades, a small needle (#9) is best. For cotton, heavier muslin, velvets, or velveteens, a medium size (#11) is suitable. For knitted fabrics, use special round-end needles designed for knits, available in various sizes for different fabric weights.

SEAMS

RAW EDGES

Q
What kind of seams should I use? And what do I do with raw seam edges?

A
Your goal should be to hide all raw seam edges. For single-layered garments like slips or dresses, use French seams for shoulder, side, underarm, and skirt back seams. Overcast raw armscye and waist seam edges with a blanket stitch or cover them with lace insertion, as French seams are not feasible there.

In double-layered garments, seams usually face each other inside the layers and are not visible, so leaving them raw is OK.

Armscye seams are typically pressed toward the bodice and hidden between the bodice's double layers. Waist seams are also concealed between the bodice layers. Any raw seams should be overcast or covered.

FRENCH

Q
Please help me with a French seam. I am a novice and unfamiliar with some sewing terms and methods for dolls' clothes. I am taking an Apprentice 1 class and want to make a Christening dress for my reproduction Baby Doll using white cotton batiste.

A
Before you begin sewing your doll's outfit, lightly spray-starch your fabric before cutting out the pattern. This will give the pieces body, making them easier to handle. For your Baby Doll, I recommend hand-stitching the small seams, as machine stitches can make them stiff.

To start a French seam, place the two edges to be sewn wrong sides together and baste them within the 3/16-inch (5mm) seam allowance. Hand-sew 1/8 inch (3mm) from the edges using small running stitches. Trim the seam close to about 1/16 inch (2mm) from the stitches and remove the basting thread.

Gently, careful not to tear the small seam open, finger-press the seam to one side. Turn the garment and fold the seam along the stitches (now right sides together) and baste again, about 1/4 inch (6mm) from the turned edge. Hand-sew a 1/8-inch seam from the folded edge and remove the basting thread.

If the seam is a side or shoulder seam, press it toward the back of the garment. For a center back seam, press it to one side. If making an opening placket in the center back, the folded French seam will lie flat in the direction of the placket, either left over right or right over left, as you prefer.

BACKSTITCHING

Q
I've been advised to backstitch at the beginning and end of certain seams. Why?

A
Backstitching is crucial, especially for seams under strain. For example, when setting a side seam in a sleeve, the underarm end of the side seam might pop open a little. Just enough to cause a bit of frustration because now you must do something about it before you can set the sleeve. Right? Alternatively, the waist end of the side seam may pop open a bit when attaching a gathered skirt to the bodice. This causes more frustration because you must do something about closing that end of the side seam before you can attach the gathered skirt. Back-stitching prevents these issues by keeping the ends of the seam closed.

Most sewing machines have a back-stitch button. To back-stitch a seam, set the machine needle about 3/16 inch (4mm) from the beginning of the seam. Hold the top and bottom thread tails, back-stitch to the seam's start, then continue stitching, back-stitching again at the end for about 3/16 inch (4mm). I back-stitch all seams every time I sew to avoid the frustration of dealing with popped-open seams. To me, sewing is a peaceful pastime, and I do everything to keep it that way. So, back-stitch regularly; it will become a habit, making sewing more enjoyable.

HEMS

TREATMENT

Q
How should I treat hems?

A
Hems can be treated in various ways, but the goal is always neatness. Sheer fabrics look nice with narrow or wide hems sewn with very small or even short machine stitches. A blind-hem stitch might look awkward. Sometimes, slightly gathered lace or narrow trim is tacked over the hem stitches on the outside.

Cotton fabrics, whether plain or printed, look good with hems sewn with small running stitches, blind hem stitches, or machine stitches. Silk skirts need a small blind-hem stitch, catching only one or two threads of the fabric on the inside of the skirt. You do not want to see any sewing threads on the outside.

Some silks and cotton with woven patterns are easy to hem with blind hem stitches, as you can catch a couple of threads inside the skirt without showing sewing threads outside. For relatively thick fabrics like wool, I avoid turning the hem edge under to prevent a bulky ridge. Instead, I hand-sew the heading of narrow lace insertion along the hem edge and tack the free edge of the lace to the inside, catching just a few threads of the skirt fabric. Alternatively, I might overcast the hem edge with a closely placed blanket stitch and tack that edge to the inside.

Rolled

Q
What is an uncomplicated way to make a rolled hem?

A
Rolled hems are very neat and so easy to make.

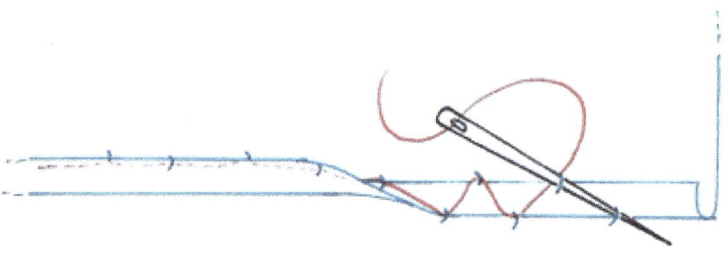

Fig.24

Start with a clean edge, ensuring all "fuzzies" are trimmed away. Fold the edge by 1/8 inch (3mm) and finger-press the fold in place. At the beginning of the folded edge, make a small stitch in the fabric smack dab next to the folded edge.

Make a second small stitch in the folded edge, about 1/8 inch downward from the first stitch.

Make a third small stitch next to the folded edge, 1/8 inch downward away from the second stitch.

Make a fourth small stitch in the folded edge, 1/8 inch downward away from the third stitch.

Continue with this "zigzag" pattern of stitches for about 2 inches, then gently but firmly pull the sewing thread up. The pulled stitches will roll the stitched edge into a neat, small, tight, rolled hem. Continue sewing in this manner until you achieve your desired length of rolled hem. This type of hem looks quite nice on the inner leg seam of split drawers, the hem edge of a ruffle, or anywhere you would like a rolled hem. *(Fig.24)*

THREADS

GATHERING

Q
The instructions that come with the pattern for my doll's dress tell me to gather the tops of the sleeves and the waist edge of the skirt but do not specify how many rows of gathering threads to sew. How many should I sew, and which threads do I pull, the top or bobbin threads? After the dress is sewn, should I remove the gathering threads or leave them in place?

A
Whether you remove gathering stitches depends on the garment's design. Some garments incorporate gathering lines as part of the design. Always pull the bottom, or bobbin, threads, which are on the wrong side. Usually, after attaching a gathered skirt or gathered sleeve caps, the gathering threads that show on the outside are removed.

If you examine the gathers after pulling the threads, you will see that the pulled side is flat with taut threads, whereas the outer side of the gathers is evenly puffed. The "flat" side is the wrong (inside) side of the garment, while the "puffed" side is the right (outside) side.

The number of rows of gathering threads you need depends on the fabric's weight. For lightweight fabric, perhaps two or three rows spaced about 1/8 inch (3mm) apart, with the first row 1/8 inch from the fabric edge, should suffice. When sewing the seam, stitch between the first two rows of gathering threads.

Medium-weight fabrics need only two rows, spaced 1/8 inch apart, with the first row 1/8 inch from the edge of the fabric. When sewing this seam, you would stitch between the two rows of gathering threads.

Heavy fabric requires three or four rows, using a heavier thread in the bobbin, with the first row 1/8 inch from the fabric edge. Heavy fabric requires at least a 1/4-inch (6mm) seam when stitching over gathers, so consider this when sewing the rows of gathering threads. Avoid sewing on top of a row of gathering threads, as they would be hard to remove.

When stitching a seam with one gathered edge, the "puffed" right-side gathers should be inside the two layers. While stitching, adjust the position of the gathers with a long pin to keep them even. After sewing the seam, gently remove any basting and gathering threads that show on the right side of the garment. If the gathering threads are to be left in place, tie them off in a firm knot on the wrong side of the garment and hide the thread ends by sewing them back through the gathering stitches for about 1/2 inch (1.2cm), trimming away the excess thread.

MACHINE VS. HAND-SEWING

Q
What thread do you recommend for machine sewing versus hand sewing?

A
It depends on the fabric and how fast you run your machine. For instance, if you sew quickly and your machine zips along at a fast pace, the needle will heat up significantly (Try sewing a fast seam, then feel the needle). Because of this, I use cotton-wrapped polyester thread for most projects. The cotton wrapping helps dispel the heat in the needle's eye, preventing the polyester fiber from melting. I also use this thread for hand sewing and on all cotton, rayon, and some silk fabrics.

Pure cotton thread is good too, but it breaks easily, and I often struggle to find the right color to match my fabrics.

For sewing trims and ribbons to silk garments, use silk thread. To prevent hand-sewing threads from knotting, run a length of it through "Thread Heaven" or a similar product, like an old-fashioned spit. It improves one's sanity.

TAILS AND TENSION

Q
As a "newbie" sewing for dolls, trying to sew small narrow seams on the sewing machine is very frustrating. The thread often gets caught, dragging the fabric down into the footplate. Once I do manage to get past this obstacle, I have trouble keeping the needle in the fabric. Please help!

A
Let us tackle the first problem: those uncooperative sewing machine threads. First, baste the seam edges together, sewing the basting threads within the seam allowance so they will not get caught in the sewing machine stitches. You want to be able to remove them easily. Basting a seam before stitching it on the sewing machine stabilizes the seam, and you won't have to worry about keeping the edges together while stitching.

To stitch a seam, position the beginning of the seam under the needle and set the needle into the fabric at the top of the seam. Lower the presser foot, grab the thread tails (top and bottom threads), and, holding them firmly, start sewing slowly. You can let go of the threads after the first few stitches. Remember to hold the threads at the beginning of every seam or edge you start to sew. No more tangled threads!

Now, the second problem: that naughty needle. Check the needle. It might not be the right size for the fabric's weight, or it may have a burr that catches in the fabric.

The upper thread tension could also be the culprit. The tension might be set a tad too tight, causing the upper thread to "grab" the fabric away from the needle. Try loosening the tension a little. The pressure on the presser foot could also cause the problem. Too much pressure causes the feed dogs to grab the fabric from underneath the presser foot and away from the needle. Try reducing the pressure slightly.

Your sewing machine manual should provide directions on adjusting both the upper thread tension and the presser foot pressure. Practice sewing seams using various tension and pressure settings on fabric scraps large enough for experimenting. You'll get the hang of it after a few trial-and-error attempts. Adjusting your skills to sewing for the smallness of dolls takes practice, practice, *practice*!

PULLING THREADS

Q
How important is it to pull threads in fabric to have a straight edge for a hem or to trim with lace? Can't one sort of eyeball the way threads lie in the fabric and cut along what one can see?

A
Pulling threads is very important if you wish to start with a clean straight edge, such as with a skirt, ruffle, or any straight-cut edge, especially when making pin-tucks. It is not hard to do. All you need is a little patience and determination. Start by cutting across just the first few threads into the selvage and begin pulling a thread along the cut. Patience is key. Pull the thread ever so gently. Don't lose your cool if it breaks. Pull out the broken thread, smoothing the puckers created while pulling the thread. Then cut the fabric along the cleared path the broken thread left, cutting just to where the thread broke. Pick up the thread with a pin and begin to pull again. Continue in this manner until you have pulled the thread straight across the fabric's width. You'll soon be an old hand at pulling threads and will wonder why you ever thought of just cutting across the fabric by "eyeballing" a straight line.

There are two end edges of a piece of fabric cut from a bolt, one of them being the leading end. This edge is the free end that was pulled from the bolt. It should be prepared by pulling a thread to ensure you have a clean straight edge, as you will use it for measuring skirts, ruffles, or any other piece of fabric that needs two straight edges. The other end edge, which was cut from the bolt, can be used for cutting out shaped pieces. I like to keep one corner of this end edge for cutting bias strips. By reserving these two edges for these different purposes, you will always have a straight edge when you need it.

HAND-SEWING LENGTH

Q
I am having an awful time with hand-sewing thread knotting while I sew. Is there some way to stop this? It always catches on pins or the edge of what I am sewing. Help!

A
I'll bet the piece of thread you are using for hand-sewing is likely too long. An 18-inch (48cm) length is ideal for hand-sewing. Yes, you will need to cut another piece of thread before you finish, but you will be happier. You could run your sewing thread through "Thread Haven." If this is not available, use a little spit. This will help prevent knotting. Try having several needles of the same size pre-threaded, so you can easily switch when one runs out, saving you the time of re-threading.

As for pins, set them so their heads are flush against the edges with their pointy ends tucked back into the fabric. This will prevent the thread from catching on them.

VARIETY OF THREADS

Q
I get so confused about all the various kinds of threads available and don't know which to use for certain projects. Could you help me out?

A
I've looked through all the spools of thread I have and found the following:

MERCERIZED COTTON
This is best for making replicas of original doll clothes, as they were often made with cotton or silk threads. However, mercerized cotton threads can be hard to find, and they don't always come in the desired color. They also break easily while sewing.

EXTRA STRONG BUTTON AND CARPET
This is mostly used for sewing buttons on large garments or upholstered cushions.

MERCERIZED COTTON-COVERED POLYESTER
This is the most popular type of thread. It is readily available, comes in a wide variety of colors, is usually hard to break while sewing, and is gentle on the sewing machine needle. These threads come in various sizes: All-Purpose for general ("normal") sewing projects, Hand Quilting and Extra Strong Hand Quilting for quilting projects, and Extra Fine for lightweight fabrics and machine embroidery projects.

Transparent Nylon

I use this for attaching a doll's little extras, such as a fan, toy, or label. It's invisible, making it look as if the doll is really holding the item.

Rayon

This might be used for topstitching or fine embroidery on a small doll's garment.

Silver and Gold Metallic

This can be used for embroidery. I use it when making a doll's fine jewelry.

Silk

I use silk threads for hand-sewing silk garments. Silk threads come in a wide variety of colors and are quite strong.

There are probably a few more out there that I am not familiar with. It might be educational for you to do some research in your local fabric and craft shops.

If you are making regular modern-type doll clothing or antique reproduction doll clothing, I would use Mercerized Cotton-Covered Polyester and Silk threads. But if you are making a true replica, try to find Mercerized Cotton thread for your sewing.

Plackets

Ordinary

Q
Please, I need some help with making a placket. Is there an uncomplicated way to make one?

A
Plackets can be complicated, but after you make one, you will see they are relatively easy to work with.

If the placket opening is an extension of a seam, follow the width of the seam allowance for your placket seam allowance. If the placket opening results from having to slash an opening, such as in the center back neck edge of a slip, place the bottom of the slashed opening a scant distance from the center of the placket strip edge. When stitching this type of placket, be careful to catch only a few threads of the fabric at the bottom of the slashed opening in the stitching.

Open out the placket opening of a garment needing one and measure the length of the opening from one end to the other. Cut a strip from your fabric a little longer than the measurement. If you want a 1/4-inch (6mm) wide placket with 3/16-inch (5mm) seam allowances, cut the strip 1 inch (3cm) wide. Pull threads, if necessary, to have clean straight edges.

Right sides together, place the right side of the placket opening over the right side of the placket strip, matching the edges, with one top end of the placket opening even with one end of the placket strip. Pin it in place. Starting at the top end, baste the two together, stitching close to the double edges and catching in the bottom end of the placket opening.

Remove the basting threads after stitching. Finger-press the seam toward the placket strip. Fold the unstitched edge of the placket strip 3/16 inch to the inside, then fold this edge over to meet the garment opening/placket strip seam stitches. Hand-tack this folded edge to the stitches.

Fold the whole placket in half from the bottom edge of the placket, matching the two top ends. Fold one end of the placket over to the wrong side so that the placket opening laps 1/4 inch left over right or right over left, your choice.

Tack the folded-over top edge in place. Press the whole placket so it lies flat.

SIMPLE

Q

Sometimes, when I am constructing a single-layered garment that has French seams, and the opening calls for a placket, I want to be lazy and not make a full placket using a placket strip. Is there a simpler, easier way to finish the opening without having to construct a placket? Some of my dolls are so small that a placket will be just too bulky.

A

Sure! And it is quite simple. When you cut the garment that requires a placket, cut the seam in which the placket is to be set a little wider than normal. For instance, when the pattern calls for the back seam to be 3/16 inch (5mm), cut a 5/16-inch (8mm) seam.

When starting to make the French seam, wrong sides together, make the first seam 3/16 inch (5mm) wide, and stitch just to where the placket opening starts, backstitching at that point. Let's consider this point as **X**. Trim the stitched seam to a scant 1/8 inch (3mm) wide just to **X**. Also, clip the seam at **X**, being careful not to clip the seam stitches.

Turn the edge, finger-pressing it, and stitch the second 1/8-inch seam, again just to **X**, backstitching again; don't clip the seam. You now have a French seam up to **X**, with two unfinished edges extending beyond **X**. These are your placket opening edges.

For your "lazy" placket, first turn the garment right-side-out, then finger-press the seam in the direction you want the opening to close; right over left or left over right. Your choice. Press just the seam toward your direction.

Working from inside the wrong side, you will see the free edges one on top of the other. Fold the bottom edge under twice to match the depth of the French seam. Hand-sew this small hem in place with small running stitches.

Fold the top edge up and over twice so it kind of matches the depth of the French seam. It may be a tad tight over **X**. Hand-sew this small hem in place. You will notice that this second hem is a little narrower than the bottom hem. This is OK.

You now have your "lazy" placket. You'll be making many more!

REALLY LAZY

There is another kind of lazy way to make a placket opening, and I make these on very small dolls as they don't create bulk.

Slash the garment where you want a placket but make that slash short. At the bottom of the slash, cut the fabric along a thread 1/4 inch (6mm) from each side of the slash. Fold the slashed edges over 1/8 inch (3mm) twice, and hand-sew them in place using very small stitches. Now, place one edge over the other, right over left or left over right, your choice. Of course, this makes a little pleat at the bottom of the "placket." This is OK. On the wrong side, tack the edges over each other at the bottom of the opening.

You could make the finished slash edges a little narrower by cutting the fabric at the bottom of the slash even shorter than 1/4 inch (6mm). Tiny is great! Tiny dolls like tiny sewing.

You'll make a lot of these, too!

PRESSING

PRESSING CLOTH

Q
I am always advised to press as I sew. Why is this so important? And why a pressing cloth?

A
Pressing has always been a crucial aspect of sewing. Seams lay flat when pressed open or, in the case of French seams, pressed to one side. Small garments, such as dolls' clothing, remain wrinkle-free when pressed during construction.

Pressing itself can eliminate puckers. If you encounter puckers, adjust the upper or lower tensions according to your machine's manual.

A pressing cloth prevents direct contact between the iron's hot soleplate and certain fabrics. Silk, wool, rayon, nylon, polyester, and any fabric with a pile should never have direct contact with an iron. Most cotton fabrics can withstand direct contact, including fine batiste, muslins, and nainsook used for dolls' garments. However, monitor the iron's temperature, as these delicate fabrics can burn easily. Often, a large cotton or linen handkerchief can serve as a pressing cloth or even a piece of batiste. You need something that allows steam to pass through to the fabric while keeping the iron's soleplate from touching it.

FINGER PRESSING

Q
OK. I'll bite. What is "finger pressing?"

A
Often, unless you have a tiny arrow-shaped iron, it is nearly impossible to get a regular-sized iron into a garment to press seams open or to one side or to press the turned edges of what you are working on. Besides, finger pressing is much more convenient.

Finger pressing involves using your fingers to press a seam open or to one side on the inside of the piece you are sewing. Run a fingernail along the seam stitches to ensure it stays open or pressed to one side. Then, turn it to the right side and finger-press along the seam stitches again. When folding edges over for hems, pressing with your fingernail along the folded edge creates a permanent fold. I finger-press all the time, mostly as a time-saving measure, as it takes time to get up from the sewing machine, position the piece on the ironing board, and press it with the iron, then return to the sewing machine. I do use the iron to press a garment as I work on it, just to keep it from getting too wrinkled as I handle it.

PLEATS
I have had several requests for an explanation of pleats. Although pleats are a relatively small part of costuming and are used almost exclusively for gathering skirts and sleeves to a waist or into an armscye, the subject can still be confusing. The main reason for the confusion lies in the difficulty of describing the process of making pleats in words. The differences among knife pleats, box pleats, rolled pleats, stacked pleats, and cartridge pleats require line-drawn illustrations to fully understand.

KNIFE PLEATS
These are the most basic types of pleats, dating back to the 6th century, and are most commonly used for gathering purposes. They produce a smooth line down from the gathering point. The classic knife pleat has a 3:1 ratio, meaning 3 inches (8cm) of fabric will make a 1-inch (3cm) pleat. There are three completed knife pleats in the drawing. The next pleat will start by folding the fabric at #11 and bringing the fold over to #13. #12 is an inside pleat fold. Clear? *(Fig.25)*

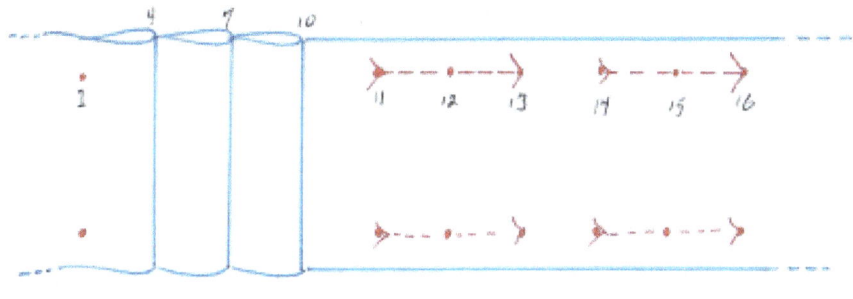

Fig.25

Box Pleats

Box pleats were very popular for Italian Renaissance and 16th-century costumes. They were used in skirts and petticoats to be worn over Bumrolls and to pleat large sleeves into armscyes. They consist of two knife pleats, back-to-back. The 3:1 ratio remains the same. These pleats tend to have more "spring" than knife pleats and tend to puff out. *(Fig.26)*

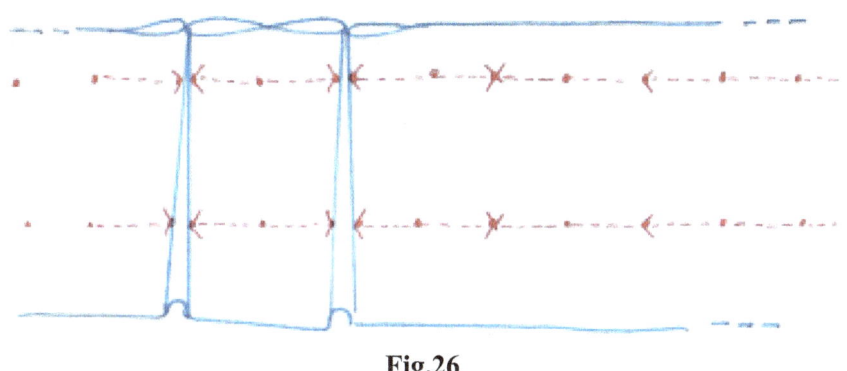

Fig.26

Stacked Pleats

Maintaining the 3:1 ratio, box pleats are "stacked" (one on top of another) where extra fullness is desired. To make a 1-inch (2.5cm) stacked box pleat, you would need 5 inches (12.7cm) of fabric. The fabric will spring out even more from a seam. These pleats create more bulk in the seams and are mostly used in creating small neck and wrist ruffles in lightweight silk, organza, or organdy. The "wrong" side of these pleats produces a nice "figure eight" ruffle. *(Fig.27)*

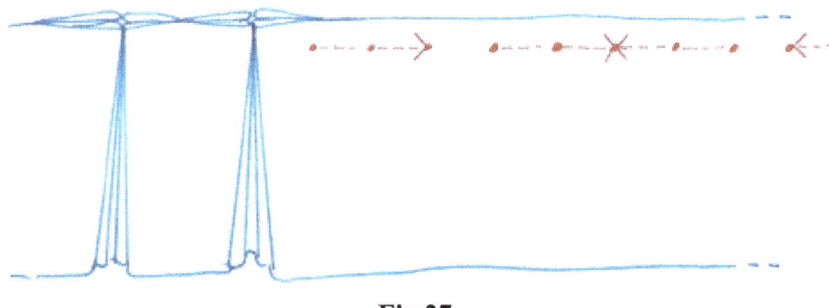

Fig.27

ROLLED PLEATS

Rolled pleats are not found commonly. They are long tubular pleats that run from the waistline to the ankle and require more fabric than box or knife pleats. The minimum amount needed for a 1-inch (3cm) rolled pleat is 5 inches (13cm) of fabric. One pinches an inch of fabric at the waist and rolls it over twice, creating a pleat with at least five layers of fabric. Rolling it over again creates seven layers.

Rolled pleats create very bulky seams. Most times, a skirt with rolled pleats has the pleated edge finished and sewn to the underside of the finished dress bodice instead of sewing a waist seam, similar to cartridge pleats.

CARTRIDGE PLEATS

Cartridge pleating is a method of gathering substantial amounts of fabric for small waistbands or shoulder armscyes without adding bulk to the seams. The fabric also springs away from the waist or shoulder more than it would with box pleats, knife pleats, or even gathering with running threads. In some 16th-century gowns, cartridge pleats nearly eliminated the need for Bumrolls.

Cartridge pleats must be sewn by hand but are worth the effort. Before starting, prepare the waist edge or sleeve edges by folding them over 2–4 inches (5cm to 10cm) to the wrong side. If the fabric is thin, a strip of wool, flannel, or other heavier fabric can be slipped inside the fold to give the pleats more body.

Starting 1/2 inch (1cm) away from the edge, sew three rows of large running stitches 1/2 inch apart across the edge, leaving long tails of thread at one end. The stitches in the second and third rows should match the placement of the stitches in the first row. If the fabric is heavy, the stitches can be anywhere from 1/2 to 1 inch long. *(Fig.28-1)*

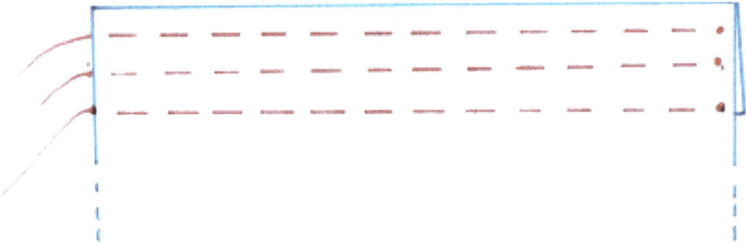

Fig.28-1

The free tails of the thread are knotted together and pulled. When the threads are drawn up, the pleats fall into an accordion pattern. *(Fig.28-2)*

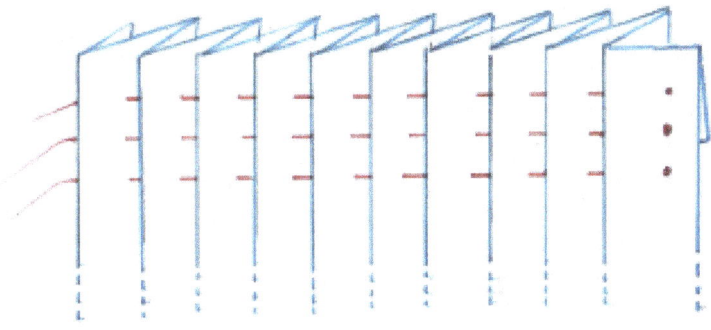

Fig.28-2

After gathering the edge to fit the waist or armscye, knot the pulling threads again to keep the pleats in place. Place the wrong side of the waistband against the pleats, and whip the pleats by hand to the waistband, catching just the tops of each pleat. The pleats fall to the wrong side of the garment. *(Fig.28-3)*

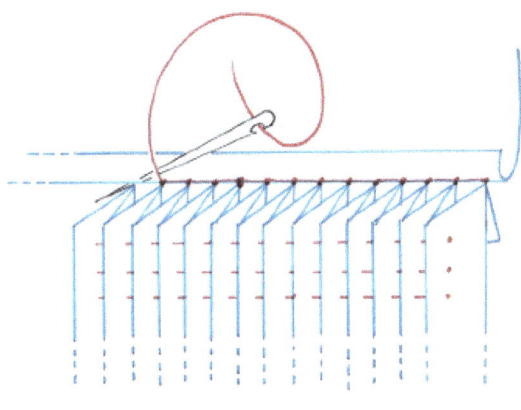

Fig.28-3

BUMROLL

OK. So, you ask, "What is a 'Bumroll'?"

A Bumroll, as its name suggests, is a roll, usually a fabric tube stuffed with horsehair, tied around the bum. It was an essential piece of Tudor and Elizabethan underwear. It was tied around the hips to make a woman's skirt swell out at the back waistline before falling to the ground. Like all items of women's fashion, it was the subject of scathing satire and clerical condemnation; nevertheless, it was used throughout the 16th century and into the 17th century and considered an essential aid to fashionable dress. A Bumroll was usually worn in conjunction with a farthingale, or hoopskirt, worn by wealthier individuals but was sometimes worn by poorer women who wished to appear fashionable.

FARTHINGALE?

Farthingales were hoop skirts worn to support heavy, full skirts. As far as I know, there were three types: the Spanish farthingale, which was cone-shaped with hoops graduating in circumference from the waist to the hem and sewn to a heavy skirt; the French farthingale, which had a pad, much like a Bumroll, added to the waist and hips area of the Spanish farthingale; and the Wheel or Drum farthingale, which was similar to the French farthingale but with larger and better padding around the hips. Look at some pictures of Elizabethan costumes, and you will see just how wide those skirts were around the hips. Wow!

TUCK 'N PRESS PLEATER

Q
How can I make even knife pleats in my doll's skirt? I have tried the measure, mark, and baste method, but the pleats seem to come out uneven, with some appearing wider than others.
A
The easiest way to make even pleats is to use a "Tuck 'n Press" pleater. Most sewing supply catalogs or large sewing supply establishments sell them. They come in several lengths and widths, allowing you to create evenly spaced, professional-looking pleats ranging from 1/4 inch to 1 inch (6mm to 3cm) or wider. They come with instructions.

Before using a Tuck 'n Press pleater, ensure you hem any skirt before pleating. You don't want to un-pleat the hem edge, make the hem, and then have to re-pleat that edge. Also, consider the space before the first pleat and the last pleat. You need fabric for a center-back seam allowance and an overlap.

PIN-TUCKS

Q
Even though I measure several times, my pin-tucks just do not look crisp and even. How can I make them straight? I want three 1/4-inch pin-tucks above a 1-inch hem in my doll's slip.

A
To achieve crisp and even pin-tucks, start by pulling threads for a clean edge. Make precise measurements when marking the fabric for the pin-tucks. You will need a ruler, tape measure, fabric marker, straight pin, and scissors.

You will need a piece of fabric that is the desired width plus enough for two 3/16-inch (5mm) center back seam allowances. The desired length must include enough for the three pin-tucks, at 3/4 inch (2cm) each, and 1–1/8 inch (3cm) for the hem.

At the top and bottom edges of the fabric piece, pull threads to create clean, straight edges. For the slip skirt hem, use the fabric marker to make a line of marks 1/8 inch (3mm) upward from and across the edge. Make another line of marks 1 inch (2cm) upward from and along the 1/8-inch marks. Fold the fabric up along these two lines to the wrong side of the fabric, finger-pressing each fold. Pin and baste the hem in place. Remove the pins. Top-stitch the hem in place, stitching close to the edge of the 1/8-inch fold. Remove the basting threads. Press the hem. Do not sew the center back seam.

On the right side of the hemmed skirt, use the fabric marker to make two lines of marks for the first pin-tuck: 1/2 inch upward from the hem stitches, then 1/4 inch upward from the 1/2-inch marks. The 1/2-inch marks are the folding line of the pin-tuck. The 1/4-inch marks are the stitching line of the pin-tuck. When stitched, open the skirt and press the pin-tuck downward toward the hem.

For the second and third pin-tucks, repeat the process, measuring from the stitching lines of the first and second pin-tucks.

Following these steps should help you create perfect pin-tucks each time. For an antique look, hand-sew the pin-tucks in place using small running stitches instead of using a sewing machine. The hem can also be hand-sewn.

On Fabrics

VELVETEEN

Q

I have been given three pieces of vintage cotton velveteen that have been stored in a trunk for several years. Even though they were carefully wrapped in acid-free tissue, with several layers of tissue inside the folds, the areas where the fabric was folded have almost permanent fold marks and are slightly faded along the folds. How can I get rid of these so that I can use the fabric for several dresses for my dolls?

A

Try pressing the fabric, right side down, on a terry cloth towel and using a pressing cloth. The towel will cushion the nap of the fabric, allowing the steam to flatten the fold mark without damaging the nap. A pressing cloth is necessary when pressing velveteen, keeping the steam iron about 2–3 inches (5cm to 8cm) above the cloth. Some fold marks might be stubborn enough to remain, and you can do nothing about the fading. Cut your pattern pieces close to or around them or disguise them inside pleats or gathers. I would never place a pattern over this fold, even if the color had not faded. The fold is almost permanent and would mar your garment piece.

TULLE

Q

I am trying to make my doll a tulle ballet costume and am having a terrible time sewing the pieces of tulle together. I always seem to end up with too much of one seam edge (usually the top one). What can I do? Also, how does one easily gather tulle to make ruffles?

A

Tulle is very bouncy and not very cooperative. Silk Illusion tulle is the easiest to sew with, while nylon tulles are the worst. The basting thread is your best friend when sewing any type of tulle. A piece of stabilizer, such as tissue paper, paper towel, or tear-away stabilizer found in most sewing supply shops, is also helpful. Facial tissue does not work well as it tears too easily. Be aware that any type of paper stabilizer will dull the point of your sewing machine needle, so you may want to discard the needle after finishing your tulle ballet dress.

Baste seam edges together using small stitches. The basting threads will give the sewing machine feed dogs something to grab besides the tulle, allowing it to slide under the presser foot easily. A stabilizer will provide an added purchase. Medium-length or long machine stitches help, too. Baste the seams together about 3/16 inch (5mm) from the edge. If it helps to keep the stabilizer in place while sewing, you could tack it along the seam edge as well.

Stitch the 3/16-inch seams, stitching on top of the small basting threads. The basting threads will not be visible as they will get lost in the machine stitches, so they needn't be removed. When you have finished sewing a seam, gently tear away the stabilizer (if used).

When gathering strips of tulle for ruffles, use two lines of small-sized hand-sewn gathering threads about 1/8 inch to 1/4 inch (3mm to 6mm) apart, with the first line 1/8 inch from the edge of the tulle. When attaching the ruffle to fabric or tulle, pin them in place, distributing the gathers evenly.

Baste the ruffle in place, sewing between the two lines of gathering threads. Remove the pins.

When stitching the ruffle in place with the machine, stitch on top of the basting threads, not forgetting to use some stabilizer as well. Again, the basting threads will not be visible, so they needn't be removed.

Sewing tulle ruffles to fabric is much easier than sewing them to another piece of tulle, as the fabric acts much like a stabilizer without having to be torn away. You may want to sew all parts of the ballet dress that are to have ruffles on them flat, then sew the seams later.

BRUSHED FELT

Q
What is "brushed felt?" I wish to make a top hat for a doll, dressing him as a gentleman, and the pattern calls for brushed felt. Can you explain?

A
According to the Oxford American Dictionary, "felt[1] (n) is a kind of cloth made by matting and pressing fibers. felt v. 1. to make or become matted together like felt. 2. to cover with felt."

To make brushed felt, the surface is brushed with a stiff brush. For your hat, a good stiff toothbrush will do the job. This will give the felt a nap. Generally, felt does not have a nap. You can do this by brushing the pieces of the top hat as you construct it.

Make the top hat with thin cardboard first, then glue the felt pieces to the cardboard shape.

Brush the felt with the brush until you start raising a nap, swirling the nap in one direction only, and smoothing it down with your fingers. Take care to brush the felt at the side/top edge and the base/brim edge of the crown to hide the "seams."

Line the crown, gluing the lining in place. Finish your top hat by binding the rim edge with a grosgrain ribbon, starting and ending at the center back edge. Fix a band of the same ribbon around the base of the crown, making a flat bow to cover the spot where the ends of the ribbon meet, usually at one side of the crown. Also, glue some of the same ribbon inside the base of the crown. Then, to really finish it off, brush the felt one more time.

Fraying Velvet Edges

Q
How do I keep velvet or velveteen from fraying and leaving minuscule bits all over me, my sewing machine, and everywhere else? And how do I keep the seams even so that I don't run out of a bottom layer before I get to the end of the seam? Also, how do I press a seam without flattening the nap?

A
There is nothing more frustrating than having to do a thorough cleanup before even starting to sew a dress together. There's really nothing you can do about those minuscule bits when cutting out a pattern. It's just one of those "things" a dressmaker accepts when working with velvet or velveteen. However, you can control them when sewing garment pieces together.

Let's tackle those minuscule bits first. After cutting out your pattern and before you start sewing, instead of using something like Fray Check™ along the edges, which can leave them a bit stiff, I discovered that spraying the wrong side of small pieces with a light mist of hair spray keeps the edges intact. Be sparing with the spray; you don't want to soak the pieces. Hold the hair spray container about 12 inches (30cm) above the pieces. Place the pieces right side down on a soft towel, pinning them in place if you wish. After spraying, allow them to dry completely. The hair spray leaves no sticky residue and often gives limp velvet a bit of body.

Now, for those uneven seams. Basting the seams together helps, but it may not prevent the top and bottom layers from becoming uneven by the end of the seam. There just might be too much pressure on the presser foot. The feed dogs will grab the fabric away from the top piece. Your sewing machine's instruction booklet will explain how to reduce the foot pressure. Your stitch length might also be too short. Try using a stitch length between eight (8) to ten (10) stitches per inch. Experiment with fabric scraps, adjusting presser foot pressure and stitch length. You might also try using a tear-away stabilizer between the feed dogs and your fabric pieces. I usually hold the bottom piece of fabric, maintaining even pressure while sewing. This helps ensure both seam edges end up the same length.

Seam Sticks

Preventing velvet or velveteen from flattening while pressing is not too difficult, especially if you press the fabric nap side down on a plush towel. Also, place seam sticks under and between the seam edges, as well under the wrong side of the garment. Seam sticks can be made out of anything. I use narrow pieces of cardboard that are just wide enough to extend slightly beyond the seam edges. They will prevent "tell-tale" signs of seam edges from appearing on the right side.

Using a damp pressing cloth is essential. Place it over the open seam. Instead of pressing the iron down onto the cloth, suspend it about 1/4 to 1/2 inch (6mm to 1cm) above the garment, just touching the open seam with the tip of the iron, allowing the steam to do most of the pressing. Remove the pressing cloth and let the fabric cool before removing it from the ironing board. After finishing the doll's garment, place it on the towel and, holding the steam iron about 6 inches above the garment, give it a shot of steam all around to raise any part of the pile that may have flattened. Using an old toothbrush along seams also helps to re-raise the nap.

On Finishing

Note: If I include a line drawing, or two with my answers, for your reference only, all pencil marks, lines, and threads in a line drawing are represented by red ink. Fabric included in a line drawing is represented by blue ink. Pen marks, lines, arrows, and words are represented by black ink.

Bias Piping

Trim

Q
I wish to make a few unlined outfits for my daughter's and her friend's 18-inch (46cm) dolls and finish the armhole and neck edges with bias piping trim. How can I do this and have the edges look finished with no raw edges in the bias piping trim?

A
Sewing for 18-inch dolls is so much fun, and bias piping trim makes an outfit look special. Creating bias piping with no raw edges is all in the technique.

1. Cut several 1–1/4 inch (4cm) wide bias strips from the fabric you want to use for the trim and sew them end-to-end, making one long strip. Ensure the cut ends of each piece are in the same direction and that all the seams are on the wrong side of the fabric.

2. Press the seams open and trim the tiny triangles of fabric along the edges. It helps if you lightly spray-starch the whole strip after sewing it together.

3. Finger-press one long edge over 3/8 inch (1cm). Finger-press the other edge over 3/8 inch, tucking that edge under the first folded edge. Press the folds in place. This is the wrong side of the strip.

4. Use a small string for your piping. Open the second fold and place the string inside, leaving a long tail sticking out of the end where you will start stitching. Do not cut the string from its source. *(Fig.29-1)*

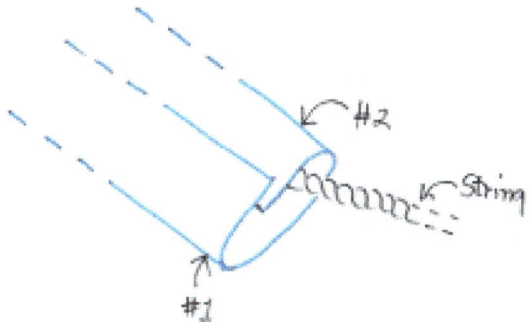

Fig.29-1

5. Close the fold over the string, keeping the string inside under the folded edge. Baste the folded edge over the string, sewing close to, but not next to, the string. Use the zipper presser foot to sew the piping. Adjust the zipper foot so the left edge of the foot is next to the machine needle. Stitch along and next to the string, being careful not to catch the string in your stitching.

6. When sewn, gently pull the piping along its length with your fingers and thumb, straightening any puckers and allowing the fabric to adjust itself along the string. This is why I advised you not to cut the string. Re-tuck the edge of the second fold under the edge of the first fold and trim the string away at each end.

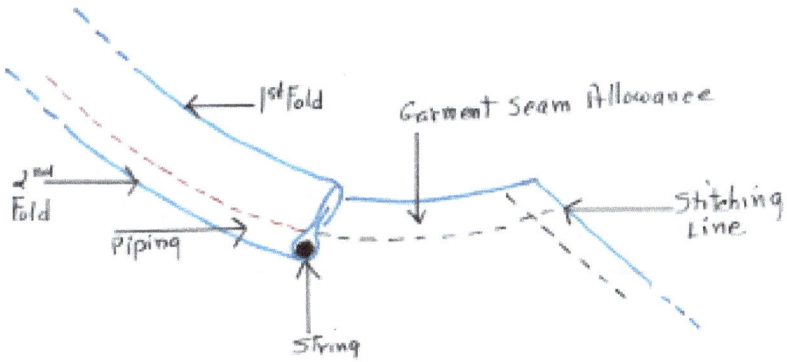

Fig.29-2

7. Place the wrong side of the piping along the right side of the edge of the garment you wish to trim, with the first fold sticking up and the piping stitches (you've just sewn) along the garment's seam stitching line. *(Fig.29-2)*

8. Pin, then baste it in place, sewing close to the piping stitches. Remove the pins. Stitch the piping to the garment, stitching along the piping stitches. Remove the basting thread. Trim the curved edge of the garment seam to about 1/8 inch (3mm). Fold the bias trim over to the wrong side and press the turned edge. See? No raw edges. The first folded edge makes a clean finished edge on the inside of the garment.

Lined

Q

How can I make piping to match the main fabric in a doll's coat? The fabric is a thin gauze-type silk with a gold thread pattern woven into it. I wish to line the coat with China silk, the same color as the coat fabric. If I use strips of thin gauze for the piping, the strands of the string that I am using to make the piping show through and look quite ugly. The string also dilutes the color of the fabric and leaves a yellow cast. Please help.

A

An interesting problem. Though I've never encountered it, I think the solution is to line the bias piping using the China silk lining.

1. Cut several 1-inch (3cm) wide bias strips from the garment fabric and the China silk to make enough piping for the edges you wish to pipe. Make two long individual strips by joining the pieces of each fabric together. Finger-press the seams open and trim away those little triangles. You want the edges to be clean.

2. Lay the right side of the China silk bias strip over the wrong side of the garment fabric bias strip and pin them together. Hand-sew the two strips together down the center with long basting stitches (this basting thread will be removed after you have made the piping).

3. Place the small string down the center of the wrong side of the double strip and fold the strip in half over the string, leaving a long trail of string at the beginning of the piping. Do not cut the string from its source. Loosely baste these edges together, sewing about 1/8 inch (3mm) from the edges.

4. Using a zipper foot, stitch close to the string inside the folded strip, being careful not to catch the string in the stitches. Do not cut the string yet.

5. When sewn, gently pull the bias along the string, smoothing out any puckers. See why I suggested not cutting the string? Trim away the string at each end. Also, trim the double edge so that you have a clean 3/16-inch (5mm) seam allowance. Gently remove the basting thread along the folded edge. There you are! Lined bias piping.

Unlined

Q

I am making a coat for my doll, and the pattern calls for bias piping around the armscyes, wrist edges, and outer edges (the neck, down the front, and around the hem). Please, I need help making the bias piping.

A

The amount of fabric you need for bias piping depends on the size of your doll. You will need at least an extra one-eighth of a yard of coat fabric for your bias piping trim. Your bias strips should be 1 to 1–1/4 inches (3–4cm) wide, depending on the thickness of the coat fabric and the width of the piping string used.

1. Before cutting fabric for your bias piping, measure around the coat's outer edges, armscyes, and wrist edges to determine the length of bias strip needed. For this project, you will need a ruler, measuring tape, a fabric marker (a white one if the fabric is dark), a few straight pins, and scissors.

2. Lay the coat fabric out on a flat surface, wrong side up. Fold one corner of the fabric up and over so the selvage edge is across the width of the fabric. The size of the fold depends on how many bias strips you need, as you will be using that triangular piece for your bias strips.

3. Finger-press the folded edge, then cut the fabric along the fold. This is a true bias cut of your fabric.

4. Mark lines 1 to 1–1/4 inches (3–4cm) wide along the cut edge of the triangular piece of fabric using the fabric marker. Measure and mark another series of the same measurements from the first marks. You will now have two (2) marked bias strips. Use a ruler to draw cutting lines through these marks.

5. Cut these two strips. Continue to measure, mark, and cut bias strips from this corner piece until you cannot cut another piece that is at least 5 inches (12cm) long. If you need more bias strips, cut them from the bias-cut edge of the coat fabric.

6. When cutting bias strips long enough to make the required length of bias piping, remember to include the addition of the 3/16-inch (5mm) seams (two to each cut bias strip), plus a little extra length "just in case" you need a bit more.

7. Lay the bias strips end-to-end, wrong side up. Some ends will be in opposite directions. Trim them so they all are in the same direction. Still with me?

8. With right sides together, pin two strips together, allowing for a 3/16-inch seam allowance. This will create a small extension on both sides. *(Fig.30-1)*

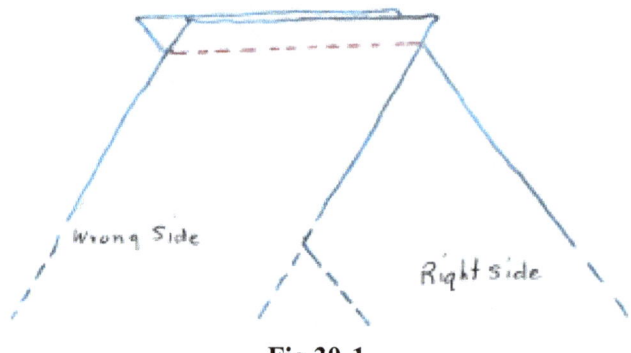

Fig.30-1

9. Continue pinning the strips together in the same way, ensuring all seams are on the wrong side. Baste these seams together and remove the pins. Before sewing, double-check that your seams are all on the wrong side. Stitch the small seams. Remove any basting threads that have not been caught in the machine stitches. Finger-press or steam press the small seams open. Trim away the small triangles, leaving the edges clean.

About the piping cord: you cannot use the piping cord sold in fabric stores as they are meant for humans and are much too large for dolls. I use plain old cotton string, which comes in many widths. Some even have a coating, making them a little stiff. I use uncoated string as it is very pliable. Be choosy when deciding which width to use. You don't want your piping so large it overshadows the coat. Catch my drift?

10. Lay the sewn-together bias strip out flat, wrong side up. Place the string of your choice down the center of the bias strip. Fold the strip in half over the string, leaving a long tail of string sticking out from the beginning of the folded-over strip. Do not cut the string from its source.

11. Baste the strip edges together, sewing near the string but not stitching into it. OK so far? Don't cut the string away yet.

12. Using the zipper presser foot of your sewing machine, adjust its placement so it is right next to the sewing machine needle but not touching it.

13. Place the basted strip under the zipper presser foot so that it and the needle are up against the string inside the fabric. Slowly stitch the bias strip seam, being careful not to sew into the string.

14. After finishing sewing the strip, use your fingers and thumb to pull the fabric along the string in both directions to smooth out any puckers, allowing the fabric to adjust itself along the string. Then cut the string away from both ends of the bias strip. See why I suggested not cutting the string?

15. Trim the seam to 3/16 inch from the stitches to the bias piping edge. You now have bias piping! Wasn't too hard, was it?

Would you like to know how to set the bias piping into the armscyes, wrists, and outer edges of the coat? OK, follow along here.

16. You've sewn the shoulder seams of the coat and pressed them open. Measure the length of the armscye seams. Cut pieces of the bias piping 1/2 inch (12mm) longer than these measurements.

17. Pin the bias piping pieces along the right side of the armscye edges, with all edges even. Baste them together, sewing through the seam allowances. Remove the pins. Clip the armscye curves (not the bias piping) slightly if necessary for easier sewing.

18. When the bias piping is on a curve, the fabric will adjust itself to the new position, and some of the string will poke out from each end. This is normal. Pull them out a little more and cut them away. The string will shrink back into the piping, leaving a small string-free space. This will reduce any extra bulk in the underarm seam. The same applies to the wrist edges and where you start sewing the piping to the outer edge.

19. Stitch the armscye bias piping in place, stitching along the bias piping stitches, being careful not to catch the string (using the zipper presser foot here is not necessary). These stitches are visible on the wrong side and will guide you in setting the sleeves into the armholes.

20. Do the same for the wrist seams and the seam around the coat's outer edge. When you've stitched the bias piping to the right side of the sleeve's wrist edges and the right side of the outer edge of the coat, the machine stitches on the wrong side will guide you in sewing the lining to the inside of the outer edge of the coat and hand-tacking the sleeve lining to the wrist edges.

21. When pinning and basting the bias strip to the outer edge of the coat, start and finish at the center back neck edge, overlapping the ends. This will leave a smooth bias piping in this area. *(Fig.30-2)*

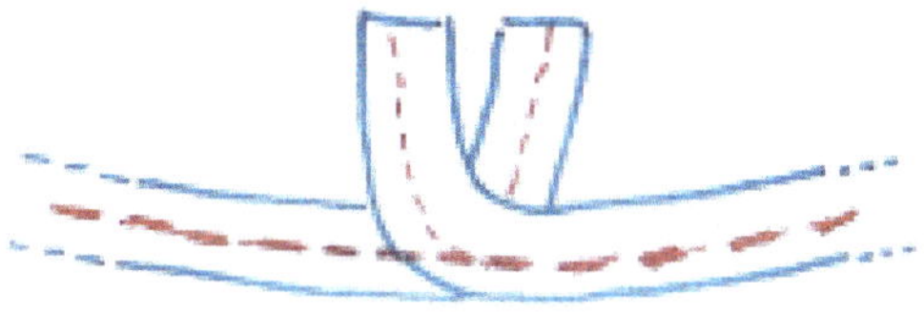

Fig.30-2

You now have a good idea of how to insert bias piping into any seam or onto any edge.

Trimming Edges

Q
I am making dolls' underwear with a single-layered bodice. How would you recommend finishing the neck and armhole edges?

A
There are several ways to treat these edges:
Trim the edges to 1/8 inch (3mm), then fold the 1/8-inch edge over to the wrong side. Press the folded edge in place.

- Use a closely placed blanket stitch in a contrasting color thread to decorate the folded edge.
- Sew a short running stitch in a contrasting color thread close to the folded edge.
- Bind the edge with lace edging.
- Hand-sew or machine-stitch scallops over the folded edge.
- Trim the untrimmed edges with flat lace edging.
- Trim the folded edges with lightly gathered lace edging.

Lace-Bound

1. Measure the neck and armhole edges and cut pieces of lace edging to these measurements, maybe adding a tad extra to each length.

2. Trim away the seam allowance of each edge. Place the lace edging on the wrong side of the trimmed edge, 1/8 inch from the edge. Hand-sew the lace in place, sewing in the lace heading.

3. Fold the lace over to the right side and hand-tack it in place. There! Nicely bound edges.

Hand-Made Scallops

1. Trim the edges to be scalloped to 1/8 inch. Fold the edges over 1/8 inch to the wrong side and press the fold in place. Working from the wrong side, use a very small running stitch to sew close to the folded edge all around the scalloped edges. These stitches will be "lost" in the scalloping.

2. Working from the wrong side, right to left, with a single strand of thread knotted at one end, start at the beginning of the edge to be scalloped. Sew three (3) small running stitches 1/8 inch from the folded edge. At the end of the third (3rd) stitch, take two (2) stitches over the folded edge into the end of the third (3rd) running stitch, pulling the thread tight but not tight enough to gather the running stitches.

3. Take three (3) more stitches 1/8 inch away from the folded edge and take two (2) stitches over the folded edge at the end of the third (3rd) stitch. Can you see the scallops?

4. Continue in this manner until all your edges have been scalloped. Press the scalloped edges from the wrong side. They look oh, so dainty.

Machine-Sewn Scallops
1. Trim the edges to be scalloped to 1/8 inch. Fold the edges over the 1/8 inch to the wrong side and press the fold in place. On the wrong side, using a very small running stitch, stitch close to the folded edge all around the edges to be scalloped. These stitches will be "lost" in the scalloping.

2. Most modern sewing machines have a built-in scallop setting. Mine has a Shell Tuck Stitch. Set the pattern so the needle inserts itself 1/8 inch from the folded edge. Tighten the top thread tension to help "pull" the fabric edge into a scallop with the zigzag motion.

   The machine "zags" off the fabric, then "zigs" back into the fabric, pulling the tight upper thread across the fabric edge, gathering the edge at that place. The machine then takes three (3) short straight stitches in the fabric, "zags" off the fabric edge, zigs back into the edge, pulling the tight upper thread. The machine continues with a zag off, zig on, three (3) stitches, zag off, zig on, three (3) stitches routine, over and over until the entire edge has been scalloped.

3. Set the beginning of one folded edge under the needle position so that the needle will zig 1/8 inch back into the folded edge. Remember to hang onto the thread tails (top and bottom threads) when the machine starts.

4. Slowly allow the machine to make its scallops, guiding the folded edge under the needle so the needle zig back into the fabric 1/8 inch from the folded edge. Continue in this manner until all edges have been scalloped.

5. When you have finished the scalloping, remember to return the top thread tension to normal. Press the scalloped edges from the wrong side. These scallops are just as dainty, but I prefer hand-sewn ones.

Cut Scallops
I have used my scallop shears to cut-scallop the neck and armhole edges of single-layered slip bodices and A-design slips. I first "drown" the edges with Frey Checkä, allowing them to become bone dry. I then use the scallop shears to cut scallops along the edges, ensuring that I use the shears correctly so I won't end up with negative scallops. If you have some scallop shears, cut a piece of scrap fabric to see what I mean by a negative scallops. I need positive scallops along these edges. When cutting the edges, the shears remove just about all the stiffened edges, leaving even scallops behind. Sometimes, with little doll dresses, I will cut-scallop the hem edge of the slips or dresses, especially dress skirts with layers of different lengths. They look, oh, so dainty.

FLAT LACE TRIM
1. Measure each edge and cut pieces of the lace edging to these measurements.

2. Pin the heading of the lace edging to the garment along the stitching line of the seam allowance, matching the lace edge with neck and armhole edges. Baste it in place, sewing in the lace heading. Remove the pins. The basting threads will get lost in the machine stitches.

3. Stitch the lace in place, stitching in the lace heading. I often zigzag over the heading to ensure the lace will not tear away. Trim away the fabric under the lace, being careful not to cut the stitching threads. Press the edges so the lace lies flat in gentle curves around the neck and armhole edges.

GATHERED LACE TRIM
1. Trim the edges to 1/8 inch. Fold the edges over 1/8 inch to the wrong side and press the fold in place. Working from the wrong side, using a very small running stitch, stitch close to the folded edge all around the edges.

2. Measure each edge and cut pieces of lace edging one and a half times these measurements. Gather the lace edging by pulling one of the threads in the lace heading to fit each edge. Hem the ends of the gathered lace to be attached to the neck edge.

3. By hand, with the gathered lace on the right side, whip the gathered lace to the folded edges, adjusting the gathers evenly as you sew. Gently pull the lace a little so it falls away from the folded edges.

FINISHING TERMS

LINING
A layer of fabric that covers the inside surface of a garment, usually separately constructed, and placed inside the garment with its right side out, giving the garment a nice finish inside.

INTERLINING
A layer of fabric that is cut the same as the garment pieces and sewn to the wrong side of the garment pieces, with the two layers treated as one. An interlining adds strength to a lighter fabric, giving it a body.

FACING
A layer of fabric that covers part of a garment, such as the open front or flap of a jacket. A face can be a contrast color to the main color of the garment.

INTERFACING

A layer of fabric that is sewn inside the garment where a facing is to be used to give this part of the garment some extra body. Sometimes, the interfacing is tacked to the facing itself using long tailor tacks, and sometimes, it is attached to the facing with heat (iron-on interfacing).

The design of a garment will tell you whether to sew the lining or interlining to each piece of the garment, treating the two layers as one, or make two separate garments and sew them together wrong-sides-in. A lining for a jacket, coat, or dress bodice is usually made to have the wrong side facing the wrong side of the jacket, coat, or dress bodice. If the sleeves are lined, they are lined separately.

Let's say you have a close-fitting jacket with several panels fitted together. Making a separate lining would be a hard fit as it wouldn't stay in place. It would tend to fall away from inside the jacket. Of course, on a doll, that does not move around much, this wouldn't be a problem. Still, it would be perfectly acceptable to leave the jacket without a separate lining. This type of jacket would have an interlining sewn to the jacket fabric pieces with each double piece treated as one. When sewn together, the raw edges of the seams would be bound or overcast. Did you know that in the "early" days, paper was used as an interlining? Interesting.

BIAS BINDING

Q

Narrow bias binding looks so dainty on a baby doll's dress, and I'd like to know how to make this type of finish. Would you enlighten me, please? Thank you!

A

This bias binding is made by folding a 1–1/4-inch (4cm) wide strip of bias in half lengthways before sewing it to the edge to be trimmed. The double edge of the folded bias would be treated as one edge.

1. Measure the neck and sleeve edges after the sleeve edges have been gathered. Cut enough 1–1/4-inch wide bias strips of the fabric you are using so that, when sewn together, they total the measurement of the sleeve and neck edges plus an additional three (3) inches.

2. Fold the strip in half lengthways and baste the edges together. Pin and baste the double bias strip to the right side of the edges to be trimmed, sewing within the 3/16-inch (5mm) seam allowance. Remove the pins.

3. Leave enough of the bias strip around the neck edge at each center back edge to fold under, about 1/4 inch (6mm). Also, leave enough of the bias strip around the sleeve edges for a 3/16-inch underarm seam allowance.

4. Stitch the 3/16-inch seams. Remove the basting threads. Trim the seams to about 1/8 inch (3mm). Fold the ends at the center back over the 1/4 inch so, when the strip is folded over on itself, the ends are inside.

5. Fold the bias strip over the 1/8-inch seam edge to the wrong side and hand-sew the folded edge to the seam stitches.

6. Finish making the dress, then fold the bias strips over the 1/8-inch sleeve edges and hand-sew the folded edges to the seam stitches. This trim does indeed look very dainty and neat.

On Lace

LACE HEADING

Q
What does "heading" mean when referring to lace? And what is the easiest way to gather or ease lace? When I try to sew a gathering thread in lace, the stitches always seem so clumsy and there are big gaps between them.

A
The term "Heading" refers to the flat edge of lace, whether it is lace edging or lace insertion. With cotton or polyester/cotton blend laces, if you look closely, you will see several straight threads woven through it. These threads are used to "gather" or ease the lace. If you take a piece of lace and pull on one of these threads, you will see what I mean. The lace gathers very cleanly and evenly along this edge with no gaps. The thread you used to pull is also quite strong and stable. You would catch this thread when you whip gathered lace to the edge of a garment or the heading of another piece of lace.

Some laces, however, do not have pulling threads in the heading. In this case, gather the lace either by machine or by hand, using small stitches. If you are not confident enough to sew a line of short machine gathering stitches in the heading without some sort of stabilizer, baste the lace to a narrow strip of stabilizer, sewing in the body of the lace to keep it "still" while stitching in the heading. You must use a new, sharp machine needle for this. If you choose to hand-gather the lace, use small running stitches. Either way, by machine or by hand, sew in the lace heading. Pull the bottom thread when machine stitching to gather the lace. If the stitches are small enough, those "gaps" will be quite small and evenly distributed.

There is another way to "gather" lace if all you wish to do is attach what appears to be slightly gathered lace to the edge of a garment. Press the lace in an outward curve away from the heading.

Place the lace, right side down, on your ironing board. Using a steam iron, press the lace, curving the edge of the lace outward away from the heading. Keep pressing the amount of lace you wish to use.

When it has cooled, pick it up, and you will see that when you straighten out the heading, the lace appears to be slightly gathered. This makes a nice finish to the neck or sleeve edges of a doll's dress or can be attached to a piece of lace insertion at the hem of a doll's slip.

Lace on Socks

Q
Could you give me an idea of how I can add lace to the top edges of my doll's socks without having it end up looking too "fluffy" when the socks are on the doll or not stretched out flat?

A
Based on experience, 100% cotton lace is the best type to use. The heading edge of most laces contains several single strands of thread, which, when pulled, will gather the lace. When buying lace for your doll's socks, consider the size of the doll when choosing the width. Most 18-inch (46cm) modern dolls would require 1/2-inch (1cm) wide lace for their socks.

1. Steam-press the tops of your doll's socks as wide as they will stretch.

2. Slightly gather some of the cotton lace by pulling one thread in the heading and hand-sew the gathered heading to the tops of your doll's socks, using a whipping stitch. Start and end at the back edge, with the ends of the lace slightly overlapping each other.

3. Place the socks in hot water to shrink them back into shape and allow them to dry on a towel. When the socks are put on the doll's feet, the tops will stretch a little, but the lace will still be gathered enough to appear just a little "fluffy."

Shaping Lace

On a Curve

Q
What is an uncomplicated way to shape lace into a curve where one only wants to attach a flat curved piece of lace to a garment's curved edges?

A
1. First, examine the lace to determine which side is the right one. Place your piece of lace, right side down, on a terry cloth towel on your ironing board.

2. For an outward curved edge, around the outside curve of a collar or short sleeve, for instance, measure the outward curved edge and cut a piece of lace edging to this measurement plus a little extra for safety. Steam press the lace in an outward curve, with the heading on the inside of the curve. Gently pull the outer edge of the lace into an outward curve as you press.

3. Right sides together, pin the heading of the lace along the garment's edge, pinning in place at equal intervals. Place the pins so their heads are at the garment's edge and the pointy ends are tucked into the garment. Whip the two edges together with a single strand of sewing thread, catching a few threads of the fabric and the edge of the heading. Remove the pins and press the lace out from the curved edge, pressing it into a neat outward curve.

4. For an inside curved edge, around the inside neck or armscye edge, for instance, measure the inside curve and cut a piece of lace edging this measurement plus a little extra for safety. Steam press the lace in an inward curve, with the heading on the outside of the curve. Gently press the lace in an inward curve away from the heading, shrinking the edge of the lace into an inward-curved shape.

5. Right sides together, pin the lace heading along the garment's edge, placing the pins so their heads are at the garment's edge and their pointy ends are tucked into the garment. Whip the two edges together with a single strand of sewing thread, again catching a few threads of the fabric and the edge of the heading. Remove the pins and press the lace out from the curved edge, pressing it into a neat inward curve.

OVAL PANELS

Q
How do I easily sew a piece of lace insertion into a curved oval shape on the front panels of my doll's dress?

A
What a neat idea. The panels will give the doll's dress an elegant appearance. For this project, you will need a clean piece of paper, a pencil, measuring tape, a fabric marker, and scissors. Remember, lace insertion has two heading edges and a right and wrong side.

1. With the pencil, draw the design of your oval shape on a piece of paper. The drawn line around the oval shape should be dark enough to be visible from under the dress panel.

2. Measure the distance around the oval shape. Cut a piece of lace insertion to this measurement plus an additional 1/4 inch (6mm). Position the dress panel you wish to sew the oval shape onto over the drawn pattern and trace the drawn oval shape with a fabric marker.

3. With the wrong side of the lace insertion against the right side of the dress panel, pin the outside heading of the lace insertion around the outline of the pattern, overlapping the ends of the lace where you started. Tack the ends together, trying to make the overlapped edges "invisible."

4. Baste the oval in place, sewing inside the heading. Remove the pins. Stitch the lace in place, stitching over the basting threads in the heading.

5. Pick up one of the pulling threads in the inside heading edge of the lace insertion at each end. A magnifier helps you find these threads, as you want to use the same pulling thread at each end of the lace. Pull both ends of this thread, gathering the inner edge of the lace insertion, and pulling it toward the center of the oval.

6. Adjust the gathers so that they are evenly distributed and the lace insertion lays flat against the panel. Tie off the pulling threads and weave them back into the heading for about 1/2 inch, then trim them away. Baste the gathered edge to the panel, then stitch in the heading of the lace, stitching over your basting thread.

7. Set the bite of the zigzag on your sewing machine to capture just the heading of each edge of the lace insertion using short-length stitches. Zigzag over each heading. Steam press the panel, placing it right side down onto a terry cloth towel.

8. Carefully, using the tips of a pair of very sharp scissors, trim the fabric away from beneath just the lace, cutting next to the zigzag stitches. And there you are. Repeat this process for as many panels as you are making in your doll's dress.

SHADOW PANELS

Shadow panels can be made in the same way, applying lace insertion and a contrasting color fabric to a dress panel to create an artistic shadow trim.

1. Decide on the shape of your shadow panel and make a drawing of it on a clean piece of paper. Place the dress panel over the drawing and trace the drawing onto the dress panel with the fabric marker.

2. Cut a piece of the contrast color fabric slightly larger than the drawn shape. Place it under the traced drawing and baste it in place, sewing around the traced line.

3. Measure the distance around the drawn shape and cut a piece of lace insertion to the same measurement plus 1/4 inch. Align one heading edge of the lace along the drawn shape, basting it in place, and sewing in the heading. Stack the ends together, trying to make the overlapped edges "invisible." Stitch in the heading of the lace, stitching over your basting threads through the two layers of fabric.

4. Pick up one of the pulling threads in the inside heading edge of the lace insertion at each end. A magnifier helps you find these threads, as you want to try to use the same pulling thread at each end of the lace. Pull both ends of this thread, gathering the inner edge of the lace insertion, to pull it toward the center of the shape.

5. Adjust the gathers so that they are evenly distributed, and the lace insertion lays flat against the panel. Tie off the pulling threads and weave them back into the heading for about 1/2 inch,

then trim them away. Baste the gathered edge to the panel, then straight stitch in the heading of the lace, stitching over your basting thread.

6. Set the bite of the zigzag of your sewing machine to capture just the heading of each edge of the lace insertion using short-length stitches. Zigzag over each heading. Steam press the panel placing it right side down onto a terry cloth towel.

7. Carefully, using the ends of a pair of very sharp scissors, trim the two layers of fabric away from beneath just the lace, cutting next to the zigzag stitches. Then, carefully trim away just the dress fabric inside the shape, cutting next to the zigzag stitches and exposing the contrast color.

And there you are. A shadow panel. I like to add some slightly gathered lace edging around the outer edge of a shadow panel for that little "extra."

ENTREDEUX

WITH RUFFLE ATTACHED

Q
I wish to sew entredeux to the hem edge of my doll's dress and then add a slightly gathered ruffle made from the same fabric as the dress. Is there an uncomplicated way to do this? My efforts look so clumsy.

A
The first thing you do is set the width of the bite and length of the stitch of the zigzag capabilities of your sewing machine. The zig (into the middle of a hole in the entredeux) and the zag (off the edge of the entredeux) should only capture one side edge of the entredeux. Also, the length of the stitches should be such that with each new zig into the entredeux, the needle enters the next new hole. It takes a little experimenting to get the right settings.

1. Right sides together, pin one edge of the untrimmed entredeux to the edge of the dress hem and baste it in place, sewing along the untrimmed edge. Remove the pins.

2. Straight stitch close to the entredeux holes with short machine stitches. Trim the edge of the entredeux and hem fabric to 1/8 inch (3mm).

3. Open out the entredeux and place the edged piece right side down on the ironing board. Steam press the 1/8-inch seam away from the entredeux (toward the hem edge).

4. Place the piece under the machine needle so it will zig into an entredeux hole and zag over the entredeux/hem edge. Zigzag the two together.

5. Sew two gathering stitching lines, 1/4 inch (6mm) apart, with the first gathering line 1/8 inch from the ruffle unhemmed edge. Pull the wrong side threads up to fit the ruffle along the dress hem edge, starting and ending at the center back of the hem and leaving enough for a narrow seam in the ruffle. Tie off the gathering threads and distribute the gathers evenly across the ruffle. Sew the narrow center back seam in the ruffle. Finger-press the seam open.

6. Right sides together, pin the gathered edge of the ruffle to the remaining fabric edge of the entredeux. Baste it in place, sewing close to the entredeux. Remove the pins. Turn the piece over so you will be stitching on the entredeux side. Straight stitch close to the entredeux with short machine stitches. Trim the edge of the entredeux and gathered edge of the ruffle to 1/8 inch.

7. Open the piece out and place it right side down on the ironing board. Steam press the 1/8-inch seam away from the entredeux (toward the ruffle). Place the piece under the machine needle so it will zig into an entredeux hole and zag over the entredeux/ruffle edge. Zigzag the two together.

There! A pretty, ruffled hem attached to the entredeux.

ATTACHED TO AN EDGE

Q
I am making a set of very fancy underwear for my doll. How do I sew entredeux to the neck and armscye edges of the slip, then add a lightly gathered lace to it? I'm a bit hesitant to sew with entredeux as I've heard it is difficult. Is it really?

A
Not true. You just need a little patience. Adding entredeux to an undergarment makes it special. Lucky Dolly.

The first thing you do is set the width of the bite and length of the stitch of the zigzag capabilities of your sewing machine. The zig (into the middle of a hole in the entredeux) and the zag (off the edge of the entredeux) should only capture one side edge of the entredeux. Also, the length of the stitches should be such that with each new zig into the entredeux, the needle enters the next new hole. It takes a little experimenting to get the right settings.

1. First, measure the edges to which you wish to sew the entredeux and cut a piece as big as the total length of the measurements plus a little extra (for safety). Clip both fabric edges of the entredeux just to the entredeux at even intervals.

2. Right sides together, pin one edge of the entredeux to the neck edge. Baste it in place, sewing along and close to the entredeux. Remove the pins. Stitch the seam, stitching close to the entredeux, and stitching over your basting thread. Trim the seam to 1/8 inch (3mm).

3. From the wrong side, press the 1/8-inch seam away from the entredeux (toward the slip). Slowly, zigzag over the turned edge, capturing the entredeux holes and the turned edge of the slip fabric.

4. Trim the clipped fabric from the free edge of the entredeux and steam-press the entredeux into an inward curve. Measure the curved neckline and cut a piece of lace edging one and a half times this measurement.

5. Locate the ends of the same pulling thread in the heading of the lace. Pull the ends, slightly gathering the lace along this thread, distributing the gathers evenly. Hand-whip the gathered edge to the free edge of the entredeux.

6. Repeat these steps for the armscye edges. Gently pull the lace out away from the edges.

As I said, "Lucky Dolly."

On Fasteners

Note: If I include a line drawing, or two, with my answers, for your reference only, all pencil marks, lines, arrows, and threads in a line drawing are represented by red ink. Fabric included in a line drawing is represented by blue ink. Pen marks, lines, and digits are represented by black ink.

History
A little history of fasteners is due here. I found some very interesting information on strings and ribbons, buttons, hooks and eyes, snaps, safety pins, zippers, and elastic in dolls' clothing.

Strings and Ribbons
Originally, strings and ribbons were used to fasten garments together or keep them in place. After other fastener types came along, ribbons began to be used for decorations and trims.

Buttons
As early as 2000 BC, buttons were discovered to be mostly decorative pieces, most with a shank, some with holes. Buttons continued to be used as decorative pieces until they gradually began to be seen as useful fasteners for clothing. Real functional buttons with buttonholes for fastening or closing clothes appeared in the 13th century; they soon became widespread with the rise of snug-fitting garments in 13th- and 14th-century Europe.

In the 16th century, button makers' guilds started to develop in France. They regulated the production of buttons, as well as passed laws regarding their use. Although buttons had already been seen as useful, they were still seen as symbols of prosperity and prestige. It wasn't until the Industrial Revolution that buttons became "popularized" and "democratized." Buttons could now be used by anyone and were mass-produced.

Hooks and Eyes
The Hook and Eye form of fastening first appeared under the name "crochet and loop" in 14th-century England. Hooks and eyes were handmade from wire until Redditch, England, became the first town to machine-manufacture them in 1643. In 1830, Henry North of New Britain, CN, was one of the pioneers in mass-producing hooks and eyes. These were made in a two-wire fashion and proved problematic as they would not hold. The Richardson & Delong Hook and Eye Company

of Philadelphia, PA, manufactured a variation in 1889, incorporating a "Delong Hump" that helped keep the hook in place. The Delong Hump was a third wire with a hump. Metal eyes were seldom used until the early 1920s; instead, hand-worked thread loops served as the "eyes."

Snap Fasteners

By the late 1890s, Snap Fasteners, or Press stubs, were invented but did not become commonly used until the early 1920s. Originally made of brass and mostly square, their name came from the sound they made when pressed together—Snap!

Safety Pins

The first Safety Pins were invented by Walter Hunt in 1849. His pin was made from a single piece of wire, coiled into a spring at one end with a separate clasp and point at the other end. This design allowed the point of the wire to be forced by the spring into the clasp, making it the first pin to have a clasp and spring action. Hunt claimed it was designed to keep fingers safe from injury, hence the name "Safety Pin." Before its invention, beauty bars or pins were used to close the back of baby gowns and older children's dresses, which is likely why you don't see any fasteners (buttons or hooks) in early or antique dolls' clothing.

Zippers

In 1851, Elias Howe invented the "Automatic, Continuous Clothing Closure," but it did not gain traction as Howe was more focused on selling his sewing machine. In 1909, Whitcomb Judson invented the "Clasp Locker" device, a complicated hook-and-eye shoe fastener that locked the automatic continuous clothing closure. This too did not succeed. Finally, in 1917, Gideon Sundback designed the perfect "Separable Fastener," complete with a slider with a lock that held together two opposing rows of metal "teeth." This is now the modern zipper.

Elastic

Elastic, though not a fastener, deserves mention. Rubber was first brought to Europe by Columbus from his voyages to the New World. Initially, it had little use as it lacked real "elasticity." It wasn't until Thomas Hancock invented elastic from rubber that it began to be used in clothing. Around the 1860s, a method was developed for making elastic thread. However, it was not widely used in waistlines or to gather the bottoms of drawers until 1900.

Loop Buttonholes

Q
Is there an uncomplicated way to make button loops? I have a terrible time trying to keep those I make in reasonable shape. They always look uneven.

A
Practice! And a lot of patience. Start with an unknotted double strand of thread, not too long or it will tangle, but not too short either, or you will run out before you finish your loop buttonhole. An

18-inch (46cm) double length is best. Again, it takes practice to decide just how long a piece of thread to use.

1. From now on, treat this double strand as a single strand. You might want to moisten the double thread to keep them together and prevent knotting. I always use a little spit. Who's going to know?

2. Use a scrap piece of the fabric you wish to make these button loops on. Fold one edge over about 1 inch and firmly crease the fold. If you are going to use 1/4-inch (6mm) wide buttons on your doll's garment, use a fabric marker to make two marks 1/4 inch apart along the folded edge.

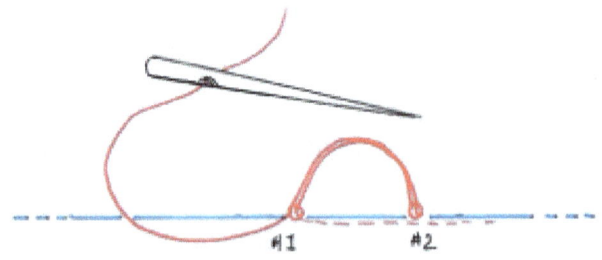

Fig.31-1

3. Along the folded edge, insert the needle about 1/2 inch (1.2cm) from the second mark, coming out of the fold at the first mark, hiding the tail of the double thread inside the fold. Insert the needle again into the fold at the first mark, pulling the thread tight. *(Fig.31-1)*

4. Insert the needle in the second mark, leaving a small loop that measures 1/4 inch from the folded edge of the fabric to the center of the loop. Make another stitch over the folded edge at that point, pulling the thread tight and anchoring the loop in place.

5. Insert the needle in the first mark, leaving the same size loop of thread, making a single stitch (you will now have four single strands of thread to work on). *(Fig.31-1)*

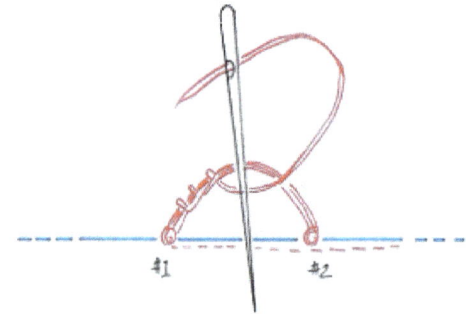

Fig.31-2

6. Using a blanket stitch, work your way over the loop until you have completely covered it. For a 1/4-inch loop, I find that I only need about eight (8) blanket stitches. *(Fig.31-2)*

7. Insert the needle into the second mark, making a small stitch over the fold, and anchoring the blanket stitches. Insert the needle once again into this same spot, coming out of the fold about 1/2 inch away from the first mark, and cut the threads.

There! A perfect loop.

There is another way to make small loops without using the buttonhole stitch. For small 1/8-inch (3mm) wide buttons, make small loops a little longer than 1/8 inch, placing them almost flat against the fold of the fabric. Use the same method as above but without the blanket stitch. Sew over the four threads four (4) to five (5) times. These loops slide nicely over the tiny buttons. Try this and see how it works for you.

On Leather And Fur

Suede Fabric

Q

I want to make a western cowgirl outfit for a doll but am not sure what to use for the skirt and vest. Would leather be an appropriate choice of "fabric?" Or a suede fabric? How would I finish the seams and hems? How would I make a fringe?

A

Considering the small size of a doll, finding leather thin and pliable enough can be challenging unless you have a reliable source. Even then, you might not find the color you want. I suggest using suede fabric, which is available in most fabric stores. Suede fabric is very soft and pliable, easy to work with, and if you cannot find the color you want, it dyes well in a cool water/dye bath.

Suede fabric has a nap and a strait of goods. The nap is much like that of velvet. When cutting out the pattern pieces, place them in line with the strait of goods, all in the same direction of the nap (either looking into it or away from it, your choice).

Unlike an active child, a doll does not move around much (on its own, anyway), so "finishing" a suede garment is quite simple. After sewing a seam, rub a fabric glue stick over the wrong side of the seam edges, firmly pressing them in place against the wrong side of the garment. If you want a hem, allow about 1/2 inch (1cm) for it and glue it in place in the same manner as you glued the seam edges.

To make the seams lie flat and give the hems clean, sharp edges, place the suede garment right-side-down on a towel-covered board. Using a pressing cloth, tap the seams and hems with the tip of a warm iron.

To make a fringe, cut a piece for fringing across the strait of goods, keeping the direction of the nap in mind (you want the fringe to match the rest of the garment). Cut the fringe in the direction of the strait of goods, leaving a narrow uncut edge along one side of the fringe strip for gluing to the garment.

After preparing your fringe, you will notice it tends to curl toward the wrong side of the suede. This is easily remedied after you have glued the fringe to the garment. Run the glue stick where you wish to place the fringe and place the uncut edge of the fringe over the glue. Press this edge firmly in place. With a pressing cloth over the garment, use the tip of a warm iron to press the fringe flat. A hot iron will melt the suede. I have one of those mini-irons and find it very useful for tasks such as this. Suede fabric is so much fun to sew with, and your Dolly will look quite nice in her Western outfit.

Rabbit Pelt

Q
I am going to make an Eskimo outfit for a doll using rabbit pelts. Could you give me instructions on how to cut and sew fur?

A
First, examine the pelts closely. You will notice that the fur falls in one direction on each pelt. For this outfit, you want the fur hairs to fall towards the doll's feet. You will need a small pair of very sharp pointed scissors to cut the fur, a black micro-Sharpie (the ink from a regular pen might bleed into the skin of the fur), and a sewing needle designed for leather. Regular sewing thread tends to cut or tear leather or fur skin, so I use thin dental floss (unflavored, of course) or thin waxed thread (usually two or three thin threads waxed together). The waxed coating is gentler on the leather or fur skin.

Remembering the direction of the fur, place the pattern pieces, all in the same direction, on the skin side of the pelts. Using the micro-Sharpie, trace the pattern onto the skin with light marks. If you have two sleeves, two fronts, or two pant legs, remember to reverse the pattern pieces before tracing them. It would be frustrating to find that you had cut out two right arms or two left fronts. To be safe, make separate reverse patterns and label them "Left Front," "Right Front," etc. For a cut-on-fold pattern piece, make two copies and tape the cut-on-fold edges together to create one piece to cut out.

After tracing the pattern on the skin side, hold the skin in your hands while you cut. Slip the tip of the scissor's upper blade along the base of the fur hairs and bang up against the skin.

Cut the fur piece with small snips, using just the pointed ends of the scissors, following the pattern tracings. This method avoids unnecessary cutting of the fur hair.

To make a seam, place the two pieces fur-to-fur and use plastic sewing clips to hold the edges together. Pins are too frustrating as they are difficult to push through leather. These clips are great.

With the leather sewing needle and a single strand of floss, sew the seam using small blanket stitches over the two edges, catching only the edges of the skin next to the fur in your stitches, not through the entire thickness of the skin. *(Fig.32)*

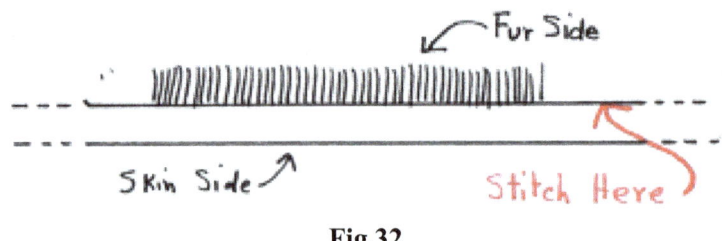

Fig.32

If you sew through the whole thickness of the skin, you will end up with an unsightly ridge that will show on the outside of your doll's outfit.

On the outside of the seams, use the same needle to "pick" out any hairs caught in the seam stitches. The seams will appear invisible. For buttonholes, slit the skin just wide enough for a small button to push through. Happy sewing!

FUR AS TRIM

Q
How do I cut a piece of fur to make a trim on the collar and cuffs of my doll's new coat? And how do I attach the trim to them?

A
Examine the piece of fur you wish to use. There is a "nap," (for lack of a better word), where the fur lies in one direction. For a trim, you want the fur to fall toward the doll's feet. You will need a short pair of very sharp pointed scissors, some clean paper, a pencil, a stick of fabric glue, a sharp needle for sewing leather, a black micro-Sharpie pen, and some thin waxed thread (dental floss will do nicely).

Trace the collar and cuff patterns on a piece of paper, marking the seam allowances. Decide how wide a trim you want. From the stitching lines of the seam allowances (not the cutting lines), measure inward on your tracings, marking the width for the trim with pencil marks. Draw a solid pencil line through these marks. Cut the patterns out along the stitching lines and your width lines. These are the patterns for creating the fur trim. Label them "Collar" and "Cuff."

Using a black micro-Sharpie, make light marks to trace the fur trim pattern piece on the skin side of the fur, remembering the fur's "nap."

Hold the fur in your hands, skin side up, and slip the tip of the scissor's upper blade along the base of the fur hairs, bang up against the skin. Cut the fur piece, little snips at a time, using just the pointed ends of the scissors, following the pattern markings on the skin side. This method avoids unnecessary cutting of the fur hair.

Rub some fabric glue on the skin side of the trim and press the fur pieces firmly onto the collar and cuffs. Stitch the fur to the garment using a single strand of waxed thread by (a) catching just the edge of the skin next to the fur. Then, (b) catch one or two threads of the garment. Repeat these two stitches until the fur is stitched in place.

Why use waxed thread? Regular thread is unkind to leather and the thin skin of furs. It cuts or tears the leather or skin when pulled to close a seam. The wax on waxed thread acts as a lubricant, guiding the thread through the leather or skin without cutting or tearing. Thin dental floss (unflavored) is also good for this type of sewing.

If you want to join pieces of fur together, place the pieces fur-to-fur (right sides in) and sew them together using a single strand of waxed thread and a small blanket stitch, catching only the edges of the skin next to the fur hair. If you try to sew through the whole thickness of the skin, you will end up with an unsightly ridge that will show on the outside of the fur.

If using faux fur for a trim, treat it the same as real fur. Faux furs are woven into knitted fabric and have a pile. Decide which way you want the pile to fall. Trace your pattern piece on the wrong side of the faux fur using a black micro-Sharpie, making light marks. Keep in mind the direction of the faux fur pile. Cut the traced pattern the same way as for real fur, cutting with the blade of the scissors right against the base of the faux fur. Use fabric glue to place the trim on your doll's garment and get it ready for sewing.

With faux fur, a thin needle and a single strand of regular thread work fine without cutting or tearing. Sew the trim onto the garment the same way as for real fur by catching a few threads of the knitted fabric on the fur side of the edge of the faux fur piece and catching one or two threads of the garment. Repeat until the faux fur piece is stitched in place. If you catch the whole edge of the knitted fabric, you will end up with an ugly stiff edge all around the faux fur piece.

PLUSH FABRIC SEAMS

Q
I am trying to make a plush toy for my grandson and am having trouble sewing the seams evenly. Please advise. Also, how can I hide the seams so they are not obvious on the right side of the toy?

A
Plush fabrics, often used for soft stuffed toys and sometimes called "fake fur," need special attention when sewing. All have a pile, much like velvet, to consider when placing cut pieces together. You want all the pieces to align with the direction of the pile.

Seam allowances are important, too. You need at least 1/4-inch (6mm) seams, and your machine stitches should be of medium length. Tension on both the upper and lower threads, as well as on the presser foot, are also important considerations. Sew a few scraps together, experimenting with stitch length and tension.

The instruction manual that comes with your sewing machine should include directions on adjusting both the upper and lower thread tensions, as well as the presser foot tension. For soft plush toys, I wouldn't recommend using a serger. When the toy is firmly stuffed, the serged seams can pull apart, exposing the stitches. Often, the seam edges will separate, revealing the stuffing inside.

Before stitching any seam, trim (clean) the "fur" away from the seam allowance. This makes it much easier to sew the seams. Pin and baste the seam edges together, sewing just inside the seam allowance. Remove the pins.

When you are satisfied with your machine settings, stitch the seams along the seam lines. Remove the basting thread. Sew all the seams required to construct your toy, leaving one seam, usually one of the back seams, partially open.

Turn the toy right-side-out and stuff it firmly, closing the opening left for stuffing.
Using a pin or needle, gently pull any fur pile that got caught in the seam stitches, fluffing it over the seams. The seams will seem to disappear, just like magic!

LEATHER SHOES (FOR DOLLS)

Q
I am trying to make a pair of leather shoes for my competition doll, but my efforts look clumsy and wrinkled at the toes. Also, when I try to sew the leather on my machine, the needle sticks in the leather, and it is hard to keep the pieces together to sew the back seam. Please help me.

A
Let's tackle the wrinkle problem first. Some instructions for making shoes suggest clipping into the edge (the width of a seam allowance) around the sole edge of the upper shoe or making V notches along this edge. These methods can be problematic for novice shoemakers, as the clipping or notching could be done too deeply into the leather. Another method involves stitching gathering stitches around the toe end of the upper, intending to pull the threads up to fit the toes around the toe end of the cardboard inner sole. Often, the pulled thread breaks, leaving you with another problem.

When I started making doll shoes, I found these instructions unhelpful and looked for another method of fitting the upper around the inner sole. I rediscovered my pinking shears and used them to cut the sole edge of the uppers when cutting out the leather pieces. The pinked edge allows the sole edge to squeeze together nicely around both the toe and heel. I also use FABRI-TAC™ permanent adhesive. Yes, it does stick to your fingers a bit, but it can be rubbed off. It does the trick a lot better than any tacky glue, which takes longer to set. When I make shoes, I make several at a time and don't want to wait for glue to set. Using FABRI-TAC™ and pinking shears alleviates the need for slow-to-cure tacky glue, clothespins, or paper clips, which can leave unwanted marks on the leather.

Using a small amount of fabric glue, place the right sides of the back edges of the shoe together. Place the edges on a piece of tear-away stabilizer, then stitch the back seam, backstitching at the beginning and end of the seam.

Before opening the seam, clip the ends of the back seam by slanting the cuts away from the ends, but not cutting into the stitching thread. Open the seam and apply a little fabric glue under the seam edges, pressing them flat against the inside the back of the shoe. Sometimes, I use a small hammer to lightly tap the seams flat.

Fit the inner sole into the bottom of the uppers about 1/8 inch (3mm) from the edge, with the center back of the inner sole aligned with the back seam of the upper.

Place a small dab of FABRI-TAC™ adhesive on the inner sole next to the back seam. Wait a couple of seconds for the adhesive to become tacky, then squeeze the back seam down onto the inner sole, holding it in place with your finger and thumb until it stays. After the heel is set, press it down on the table with your finger inside the back of the shoe. This will flatten the leather nicely around the bottom of the heel.

Ease the leather around the toe with another dab of adhesive, pinching the leather to the cardboard with your fingers. You will see how the pinked edge eases together. When the toe is set, use more adhesive to set the sides, pinching them in place until they are set.

When all the edges are set, push a finger into the toe, moving it around inside to round it out nicely. This also lifts the leather upper away from the inner sole if any adhesive finds its way inside the shoe.

You should always have a filler to fit inside the glued edges on the bottom of the inner sole so that the outer sole will not have a dent in the center. Make a pattern for the filler using the inner sole pattern, making your filler 3/16 inch (5mm) smaller all around. Cut a filler from the leather you are using for the shoe upper. This will fit nicely in the center of the set edges, making the bottom evenly flat. Using the adhesive, set the outer sole to the bottom of the shoe, pinching it all around the edges for a tight fit as the adhesive sets.

Now, let's address the sewing problem with your machine. When sewing leather, it is always a good idea to use sewing machine needles designed for leather. These needles have specially designed points that cut into the leather, easily carrying the sewing thread into stitches. They won't stick in the leather, causing a problem. It is also advisable to use a tear-away stabilizer when sewing leather. You can find them in most sewing supply stores. This material allows you to guide the leather under the presser foot, and the feed dogs grab it easily. Also, you can keep seam edges together much more easily when using a tear-away sheet. Just tear a big enough sheet from the roll for the shoes you are making. I use a thin rub of fabric glue stick to keep the seam edges together. They easily come apart so I can open and finger-press the seam open.

I like to sew a row of stitches around the upper edge of the shoe and use a piece of paper stabilizer for that. I do this before I sew the center back seam. The stabilizer keeps the leather under the presser foot. These stitches make a nice finish, and if I want to make a blanket stitch trim around the top edge, the stitches provide a nice base around which to make the blanket stitch. Also, any small trim that I want to glue around the top edge will stick better, as the glue will bond the trim to the stitches.

Off The Cuff

Tips and tricks I thought of while sewing for my clients' and my own dolls.

Sewing Silk
When sewing silk fabrics, finger-press the seams open using a fingernail, then steam-press them open. Silk is quite bouncy, and trying to press seams open without first preparing them is nearly impossible.

Cut-on-Fold
Mark all cut-on-fold lines on a pattern with **red** ink. This helps you remember to cut only one piece on a fold, instead of two separate pieces.

Using Spray-Starch
Lightly spray-starch pattern pieces cut from batiste or nainsook to give them substance, making them easier to handle while sewing, folding edges, or finger-pressing seams.

Use That Thimble
Get in the habit of using a thimble! No one wants tiny brown stains on doll clothes or sore fingers.

Hydrogen Peroxide
Keep a small bottle of hydrogen peroxide and a few cotton swabs near your sewing machine or sewing table. If a pricked finger leaves tiny drops of blood behind, dip a cotton swab into the peroxide and dab it onto the stains. They disappear like magic. Also, use the peroxide to disinfect your finger.

Pattern Notches
Cut pattern notches away from the pattern edge instead of into the seam allowance. This way, you won't risk cutting into the stitching line path. Better still, mark the notches with a fabric marker or place a pin at the notch mark.

Pin and Baste
If you are a novice sewer, pin and baste seam edges together before sewing them by machine. Basting helps keep edges even, preventing one side of a seam from becoming longer than the other.

Additionally, it ensures that one side of the seam does not end up narrower when pressed open. Been there, done that.

Favorite Music
Play some of your favorite music while sewing to keep yourself relaxed and happy, even during frustrating moments. Remember, sewing for dolls is supposed to be fun.

Changing Needles
Change your sewing machine needle often, discarding the used ones. If you sew frequently, the needles become dull and can bend when they hit pins, creating minuscule "burrs" that "pick" the fine threads of your fabrics.

Pinking Shears for Soles
If you make your own dolls' shoes, use pinking shears to cut around the sole edges instead of clipping them. Clipping can sometimes go too deep, but pinked edges "ease" more smoothly without overlapping.

Ironing Board Protection
When using spray-starch to give fabrics body, place an old sheet under the fabric while ironing. This keeps the pad of your ironing board clean. Also, keep a wet cloth handy to rub your hot iron against when ironing still-wet starched items. This removes any dried starch that collects on the iron's soleplate.

Thread Length
When hand sewing, consider the length of the thread before cutting it. Too long a thread will tangle or get caught around pins, while too short a thread may run out of thread before you finish sewing. About 18 inches (46cm) is a safe length. Spit is a particularly good anti-knotting agent and is always on hand. A thimble is also helpful to have handy.

Hiding Pin Heads
When attaching the trim to the edge of a garment, avoid frustration by pushing the pins well into the edge of the garment with their heads at the edge and the pointed ends "hidden" in the garment. This prevents the sewing thread from catching on the pins.

Dollhouse Doll Sewing
When hemming a dollhouse doll's skirt, try finger-pressing the hem folded edge instead of sewing it. Visible finishing stitches on dollhouse garments look out of place, no matter how tiny they are. Dollhouse dolls don't move much, so their hems won't fall out.

Third Hand
Did you know that your sewing machine needle combined with the presser foot can act as a third hand? Try it when you need extra help, such as when ripping a seam or weaving small, braided trims.

Magnifying Glass
You'd be amazed at how a magnifying glass can significantly reduce eye strain when doing fine hand sewing.

No Rust Here
Remove old metal hooks, eyes, snaps, and buttons from vintage dolls' clothing before laundering to prevent ugly rust stains from developing on those fragile and delicate fabrics.

Washing Hands
Wash your hands often when sewing, especially hand sewing. Your hands can leave sweat and oil on fabrics and thread, even if you're not aware of it.

Terry Cloth for Lace
A piece of clean terry cloth is good for pressing lace. Place the lace right side down on the cloth and steam press the wrong side. This makes the woven pattern on the right side "pop" out and become more visible.

Serger Trims
If you have a serger, use spools of different colored threads to create neat, fine trims by running lengths of stitches from the needles.

Your Big Toe
Your big toe is the best tool for controlling your sewing machine speed, especially when doing one stitch at a time. Try it; it doesn't take long to get the hang of.

Bias Fabric Sashes
Fabric sashes cut on the bias will fold, drape, and hang better.

Alternating Hooks and Eyes
A long edge-to-edge back closure will close more securely without gaps if you alternate the hooks and loops down each side of the closure.

Wrapping Spray-Starched Pieces
When lightly spray-starching garment pieces before construction, place the cut pieces on a small towel, spray them liberally with starch, then wrap them loosely in the towel. The towel absorbs excess starch and distributes it evenly, preventing the iron's soleplate from sticking to the fabric.

Full Needles at the Ready
If you dislike stopping to re-thread your needle, have several needles threaded with the same thread "standing" ready in your pin cushion.

Don't Like Making Knots?
If you don't like knotting the tail end of your hand-sewing thread, "hide" the tail end in the fabric at the beginning of your sewing. Take two small stitches, one atop the other, and then continue sewing. Tie off the other end of the thread when you have finished sewing by making another two small stitches and "hiding" that end in the fabric as well.

Less Lace is Better
Slightly gathered lace is much easier to sew to an edge than heavily gathered lace.

Ribbon Curls
By pulling silk ribbon over the edge of your scissors, as you would with paper ribbon for decorating packages, you can create lovely silk ribbon curls for trims and decorations on dainty dresses and bonnets.

Naked Dolls in Stands
When placing a naked doll in a stand, place a piece of soft tissue between the support ring and the body to prevent the body from being marred by the support ring.

Gluing Lambskin Wigs
A dollmaking hint: When gluing a lambskin wig onto a porcelain head, rub a thin layer of white glue on the porcelain around the edge of the skin. Pull a few hairs from the wig over the glued area to give the wig a more natural appearance. For a mustache, cut the hairs or curls off the skin and glue them to the porcelain.

Vinegar Sets Dyes
When tea or coffee dyeing, don't forget to add that teaspoon of vinegar to the dye solution to set the color.

Sewing Scissors vs. Paper Scissors
Keep sewing scissors for fabric and paper scissors for paper. Mixing them will dull your sewing scissors and may even cause nicks, making it frustrating to cut fine fabrics.

Sewing Needles for Leather
When sewing leather, use a hand-sewing needle designed for leather. It will go through the leather like a warm knife through cold butter.

Cleaning Feed Dogs
Keep the feed dogs free of accumulated fluff they pick up from fabrics while it is moving between the presser foot and throat plate. This prevents ugly bits of fluff from being sewn into your stitches.

No Pressing Lace
When washing or soaking old lace to remove dust or stains, rinse well under cold running water. Then plaster the wet lace, right side out, against a mirror or around a large glass jar to dry. This eliminates the need for pressing.

Emery Board Revisited
If fine fabrics snag on a rough patch on your fingers or fingernails, use an emery board to smooth the rough patch. Always keep an emery board in your sewing tool jar.

Keeping Pins Clean
Clean your straight pins occasionally to make them slide more easily into the fabric. Soak them in rubbing alcohol for a few minutes, then take out a few at a time and rub them with a small rag. Allow them to dry completely before placing them back in their container.

Sewing Pins vs. Craft Pins
Speaking of pins, do you do crafts as well as sewing for your dolls? And do you use the same pins for both? That's not advisable. Use separate containers for your pins to avoid picking up a pin with glue residue and using it on silk. Magnified pin holders are terrific for this purpose.

Thin Silk Pins are the Best
Regarding pins, I have found that long, thin, very sharp silk pins are the best. They easily slide into fabric and don't leave marks when removed.

Leather Finger Guard
When hand-sewing tiny garments, such as those for a Mignonette or a Doll House Doll, use a leather finger guard on the finger you sew against. This will prevent pricked, sore, and bloody fingers.

Spray-Starch Fabric First
When making tiny garments from muslin or fabric that could use a little starch, spray-starch the fabric first, then cut out the pattern pieces. Tiny garment pieces tend to stick to an iron's soleplate when ironing them dry after starching if they remain on the ironing board at all. The blast from the spray can often send them flying, mostly to places where you cannot find them.

Fray check for Hand-Made Buttonholes
A little dab of fray check along the place where you will cut for a buttonhole makes the cut edges just stiff enough to sew a nice, even buttonhole stitch over them.

Fabric Glue is Great!
A stick of fabric glue is great for holding pieces together or in place for hand-sewing, where the thread might entangle itself around pins.

Damp Pins Don't Work
If you hold pins in your mouth, be aware that damp pins do not go into fabric readily.

Long 3-inch Pearl Head Pins
Long, 3-inch pearl head pins are great for picking threads and pulling out turned corners. Their rounded ends are less likely to tear fabric threads compared to straight pins or needles.

Small String for Doll Piping
When making piping for a small doll's outfit, use a small string and cut the bias about 3/4 inch wide. Trim the seam edges of the piping to about 3/16 inch (5mm) wide.

Fray Check Soothes Frustrations
A little Dritz® Fray Check can greatly reduce frustrations with fraying edges while sewing. Run the edge of the fabric through a drop of liquid at the end of the applicator instead of applying it directly to the edge with the applicator.

Piping for Finishing
Including piping in the seams of necklines, hems, sleeves, and center back or front edges will give a more professional finish.

Outer Garments OVER Undergarments
For a proper fit, make measurements for outer garments. Ensure this is done while the doll is wearing a full set of underwear.

No Wring, No Wrinkle
When dyeing fabric, avoid wringing it out during the dyeing and rinsing process to prevent permanent wrinkles.

Dyeing Feathers
When dyeing feathers, place them on a small towel after dipping them into the dye bath. This helps them retain their shape while drying.

Small Brush for Machine Embroidering
When doing a lot of machine embroidery, keep a small brush handy to remove thread lint from the sewing machine needle and upper thread. Accumulated lint can interfere with the needle and thread, often causing the thread to break, which always seems to happen in the middle of an intricate pattern.

Rulers Make Even Bias
Using a ruler and a fabric marker to measure and mark bias strips ensures even strips for sewing.

Doll-Sized Buttons
Consider the size of the doll when choosing button sizes. Tiny dolls need tiny buttons.

Charlotte is a wife, a mother, a Doctor of Dollmaking, and an entrepreneur. A curious and industrious individual, she has been an avid reader since her teenage years and has never allowed challenges hinder her pursuits.

Although *Charlotte's Strip* is her debut full-length book, she is not new to writing, as she has contributed several articles to the Doll Artisan Guild magazine, primarily focusing on the reproduction of an antique doll's attire, as well as pieces for Doll Reader and Doll Crafter.

Charlotte operates a renowned dolls' couture business and specializes in the restoration and repair of antique and vintage dolls. Her passion for dollmaking extends to teaching others the craft.

She lives with her wonderfully diverse family in the USA.

www.ingramcontent.com/pod-product-compliance
Lightning Source LLC
Chambersburg PA
CBHW081354230426
43667CB00017B/2830